MW01505834

PROMPTING
MADE SIMPLE

HOW TO USE CHATGPT AND UNLOCK THE POWER OF AI

RAJEEV KAPUR

RINITY
MEDIA
LOS ANGELES

PROMPTING MADE SIMPLE
How to Use ChatGPT and Unlock the Power of AI
Rajeev Kapur

Published by:
Rinity Media, Los Angeles, California

Copyeditor: Russell Santana, E4 Editorial Services, www.e4editorial.com Index: Russell Santana, E4 Editorial Services, www.e4editorial.com Cover design: Yvonne Parks, Pear Creative, www.pearcreative.ca
Interior design and layout: Yvonne Parks, Pear Creative, www.pearcreative.ca
Proofreader: Clarisa Marcee

Library of Congress Control Number: 2025903232
Publisher's Cataloging-in-Publication
(Provided by Cassidy Cataloguing Services, Inc.)

Names: Kapur, Rajeev, author.
Title: Prompting made simple : how to use ChatGPT and unlock the power of AI / Rajeev Kapur.
Description: Los Angeles : Rinity Media, [2025] | Series: Kapur, Rajeev. Making AI simple for everyone. | Includes bibliographical references and index.
Identifiers: LCCN: 2025903232 | ISBN: 9781962017060 (paperback) | 9781962017077 (Kindle) | 9781962017084 (ePub)
Subjects: LCSH: ChatGPT. | Artificial intelligence. | User interfaces (Computer systems) | Natural language processing (Computer science) | COMPUTERS / Artificial Intelligence / Natural Language Processing. biscash | BISAC: COMPUTERS / User Interfaces. | EDUCATION / Computers & Technology.
Classification: LCC: Q335 .K362 2025 | DDC: 006.3--dc23

CONTENTS

FOREWORD

When you meet Rajeev Kapur—even just through his words—you immediately sense a rare fusion of pragmatism and intellect. He is not simply an expert in AI; he is a translator of its *potential*, a bridge between emerging technology and everyday understanding. With *Prompting Made Simple*, Rajeev once again invites us into that uniquely accessible space he creates: where clarity and possibility meet.

I've had the privilege of observing Rajeev's leadership journey across the ever-changing technological landscape for years, but it's not his resume or success that commands respect. It's his relentless *curiosity*, his drive to make AI not only accessible for everyone, but profoundly human-centered. Rajeev does not succumb to the hype around AI—he's invested in its utility to transform people, businesses, and communities. And he's obsessed, in the best way, with empowering others to harness it well.

That obsession is what powers this book.

Whether you're a seasoned technologist, a curious leader, or a total newcomer to AI, you will find value in these pages. More importantly, you'll find a guide you can trust. Rajeev is not here to dazzle or intimidate; he is a catalyst for our own connection to the power of AI.

Raymond Watt
YPO Global Chairman Emeritus (2024–2025)
CEO Omnislash, Inc.

INTRODUCTION

GENERATIVE AI AND PROMPTS

"AI is neither good nor evil. It's a tool.
It's a technology for us to use."

OREN ETZIONI

Every single day, generative AI solutions like ChatGPT are having a bigger and bigger impact on our lives—even when it comes to getting a burger on the run.

The fast-food chain Wendy's is working to create a seamless AI ordering process in their drive-throughs by partnering with Google Cloud. Because an overwhelming number of Wendy's customers never enter the restaurant itself (75 to 80 percent use the drive-through), the burger chain is trying to free up more of its employee resources by letting generative AI do the heavy lifting. The Wendy's FreshAI automated drive-through ordering system is intended to feel as natural as interacting with staff, providing quick answers to customer questions and taking accurate food orders—even if the customer isn't providing accurate menu names. For example, if a customer asks for a large chocolate milkshake, the AI corrects for that and knows to place an order for a large chocolate Frosty instead. They are also testing a system that allows customers to order in Spanish. And their AI initiative extends beyond the drive-through window: Wendy's will soon be using autonomous robots to transport meals underground in seconds to what the chain is calling "Carside Instant Pickup portals." Those robots will have built-in temperature-controlled delivery technology to keep fries hot and crispy.[1]

So, yes, when AI has reached the point where it's being employed to keep our french fries hot, you know it's here to stay.

The truth is no one questioned that AI generative intelligence would have a profound impact on all our lives when it was first released to the public in late 2022. As the science fiction writer Arthur C. Clarke once said, "Any sufficiently advanced technology is indistinguishable from magic." And that's what AI seems like when you first try it out—magic.

Think about it. Suddenly, we all had at our fingertips technology that could create music, images, and videos customized to our specifications. It could also compose essays, stories, poems, whatever text-based output you were after. Complex and time-consuming research? Now a snap, easily completed in minutes without breaking a sweat. In my position as a business leader, I immediately wanted to understand this game-changing technology. Once I did, I decided to share my knowledge, and in 2023, I wrote the first edition of *AI Made Simple*. In that book, I shared information about the leading AI apps, ethical concerns about the technology, and everything you can

---

1 https://www.wendys.com/blog/how-wendys-using-ai-restaurant-innovation

accomplish with generative artificial intelligence.[2] Since then, the use of AI has exploded across the globe. Here are a few 2024 statistics that make it clear that generative artificial intelligence is now embedded in our culture and in how we do business:[3]

- The AI market is expected to reach $1,339 billion by 2030
- AI will contribute an estimated 21% net increase to the United States GDP (gross domestic product) by 2030
- 64% of businesses expect AI to increase productivity
- Half of US mobile users use voice search every day
- AI is expected to see an annual growth rate of 36.6% from 2023 to 2030
- 72% of businesses have adopted AI for at least one business function

Those numbers are pretty staggering and demonstrate the startling speed with which both organizations and individuals have adopted AI into their everyday lives. If you're reading this book and still think AI really isn't having an impact on your life, let me take a moment and list the ways people are using AI without even knowing it.

1. If you use Apple's Siri, Google Assistant, or Amazon's Alexa, those **virtual helpers** are all based in AI tech.

2. **Taking a photo** with your smartphone? Well, most of the cameras built into them use AI-enhanced photo processing for better image quality.

---

2 There is an updated edition of the book now available at https://a.co/d/cnsukXA. This book is meant to serve as a companion to it.

3 https://www.forbes.com/advisor/business/ai-statistics/

3. Is your bank calling or texting you because they've detected a possible **case of fraud** with your account? Usually, AI is what flagged the problematic transaction.

4. When you shop on major online sites, you are probably fed a steady stream of **recommendations** for products similar to what you've bought in the past. Same thing with streaming movies and TV shows—Netflix, Disney+, and the like also suggest content that resembles your previous choices.

5. Scheduling an **Uber** or another ride-sharing service? AI is at play here. It works behind the scenes to optimize routes and set pricing on demand. Also, **Google and Apple Maps** are both AI-based.

6. **Chatbots** are frequently all AI. Which can be as frustrating as helpful.

7. If you're on **social media**, the algorithms that create your feed are all AI. These platforms also use image recognition software to tag photos.

8. Most **gaming, education, and training** apps use AI, including language apps like Duolingo as well as health and fitness apps.

9. Shop on Amazon or have a Netflix account? The products and show recommendations they provide are all AI generated and trained by how you shop and watch.

10. Finally, **credit scoring models** use artificial intelligence to assess the creditworthiness of borrowers.

I could go on and on. For example, AI speech recognition software can transcribe meetings, interviews, and calls in a matter of minutes. Employers use AI to screen resumes, and landlords use it to screen potential tenants. Sales teams use it to qualify leads. AI also guides self-driving cars and beverage carts. Do business globally and your customer speaks a different language? In the future, AI will translate full conversations both written and spoken in real time, true *Star Trek* tech coming our way. However, the technology does have its limitations. AI still can't take the dog out for a pee, change a baby's diaper, brush your teeth, or do your laundry—for now. Don't be surprised if all that happens soon!

In fact, Google is on the verge of releasing an ambitious new AI product that will begin to combine tasks in a one-stop app. Project Jarvis is an innovative "computer-using agent" AI designed to revolutionize the way we interact with technology, promising to handle mundane tasks and enhance our digital experiences in unprecedented ways. Unlike today's AI assistants, which respond to commands, Jarvis is designed to autonomously navigate your web browser, make decisions, and perform tasks on your behalf. Whether it's managing your emails, conducting research, or even booking appointments, this AI aims to aggressively take on a significant portion of the cognitive load that comes with digital life. Instead of waiting to be told what to do, Jarvis will actively perform tasks in real time, making the technology feel more intuitive and less like a set of individual AI tools, hopefully delivering a more seamless user experience.[4]

There's no question that AI has continued to make incredible progress since that 2022 release. The following are several specific ways that's happened.

Enhanced Language Models: LLMs (Large Language Models), the foundation of all chatbots like ChatGPT, are quickly becoming more sophisticated. The result is the introduction of GPT-4 in March 2023, which offered improved reliability, creativity, and

---

4   https://yourstory.com/2024/09/google-project-jarvis-ai-assistant

the ability to manage more nuanced instructions compared to its predecessor, GPT-3.5.

AI-Powered Search Engines: OpenAI launched SearchGPT in July 2024, an AI-driven search engine designed to provide conversational answers and relevant links, positioning it as a competitor to traditional search platforms like Google. The integration of AI into search engines has transformed information retrieval, altering traditional search dynamics. Speaking of Google, you may have noticed that when you do a search now, you see an AI summary first, which is powered by their Gemini AI engine, a competitor to ChatGPT.

Voice and Multimodal Interactions: In September 2023, OpenAI enhanced ChatGPT to support voice interactions and image inputs, enabling more natural and versatile user engagements (try it on the Open AI ChatGPT mobile App, it's terrific).

AI Integration in Robotics: Remember Wendy's automated robot delivery system? It's based in AI, which is being integrated into robotics, enabling machines to comprehend and navigate the physical world with human-like understanding. So, maybe you won't have to get up early to take out the dog in the morning after all; maybe a robot will do it for you—if the pup isn't too perplexed by what's holding its leash.

All these advancements are meant to help AI achieve its ultimate goal: the ability to engage in human interactions so we can work with it more easily. At the moment, that's not quite the case. I tend to think of AI as a comedian doing an impersonation of a president or movie star—they're trying to sound like the people they're copycatting, they're even going to contort their face and body to resemble them, but, at the end of the day, they are *not* that person. Similarly, we've programmed AI to pretend it's human, even though it's definitely not (at least not yet), lacking in several important human qualities such as the following:

- **Thinking**

  We use memory, perception, and creativity in our thinking, which AI lacks. We also can think critically. However, AI can mimic our cognitive processes of learning and problem-solving—and, with the right algorithms, training, and set rules, it can surpass our limitations in these critical areas.

- **Feeling**

  Most of us experience love, fear, sadness, anger, and empathy to the point where emotions may outweigh logic. AI doesn't have that problem. It doesn't have feelings, but it can be taught to emulate aspects of them, if that's any comfort.

- **Common sense**

  Common sense is the ability to understand, perceive, and judge things through life experiences that are shared by most people. Well, AI obviously doesn't have those life experiences. It's a glorified computer program that might mistake a white shirt for a white wall, because it just doesn't know any better. Besides not being able to make distinctions that would be a snap for most people, AI also has no experience in the physical world. It only knows what we tell it.

Sure, it'd be nice if all those human qualities were present in AI. But we should be glad that other ones are missing. For example, AI can't feel stressed or exhausted. It won't get resentful or angry with you. You also can't offend AI (even though most solutions like ChatGPT understand what *is* offensive) and you don't have to worry about being polite, because, frankly, it couldn't care less if you say "please" or "thank you." And make no mistake about it, communicating with an AI app can be easier than talking to a person, because you never have to worry about how it's feeling. With that being said, I have made it a habit of being nice whenever possible; it helps me to mentally feel like I am not talking to an AI algorithm. Plus, if the AI Terminators ever come for us, hopefully they will remember I was nice to them.

For my part, working on this new book made me realize just how much ChatGPT has been improved over the past year or so. It no longer makes as many mistakes as it used to. Nevertheless, getting what you want out of it can still be hit and miss. Which brings me to the purpose of this latest book. Because AI is quite literally everywhere and we're all working with it (whether we know it or not), I feel it's time to drill down on the details of how to get the most out of AI, in particular generative AI, by learning how to communicate with it more effectively. There is an art to it and, once you master it, you'll find yourself getting less frustrated and being more productive by getting what you're asking for faster and more accurately.

Currently, many users find themselves stumbling around and not getting exactly what they want, even though the AI app they're using may have an incredible wealth of information, images, and other media to draw from. I've designed this book for those of you who are just starting your AI journey, to help you avoid those negative experiences with AI. As the quote at the beginning of this introduction indicates, AI is just a tool. But tools must be mastered to be used effectively. With that in mind, *Prompting Made Simple* will provide you with an easy guide on how to "talk" to AI in a way it understands so it can deliver exactly what you want.

With that in mind, please understand that I didn't write this book for advanced AI users, programmers, or prompt engineers. This book is for those who are still learning how AI works and how to leverage its power. You should also note that this book focuses solely on using prompts with ChatGPT from Open AI (the company that owns ChatGPT); however, prompting is essentially the same when using competing Gen AI platforms such as Gemini and Claude.

There's an old business catchphrase: "Always ask for the sale." In other words, when you want something from someone, you need to ask for it directly. AI is no different, except that you have to ask for what you want in specific ways that make the most sense to the AI app. As I hope I've made clear, AI isn't human, even though it's been programmed to behave like one. But you can have fun with that quality and even get AI to respond as the kind of personality you want to engage with. We'll get more into that later.

You don't have to be a tech wizard to master using AI. You don't have to be a computer genius. You just have to observe certain guidelines that help AI understand your objectives. And that's not really difficult. After all, I'm sure there are a lot of people in your life that have different communication styles. And I'm also sure that, as you got to know them, you found yourself tailoring what you said and how you said it to each of them so you could have the most productive interactions. You obviously don't talk the same way to, say, a boss as you would a romantic partner or your child or even a pet—that could lead to disaster, embarrassment, or your dog cocking its head at you in confusion. No, what usually happens is you learn everyone's individual communication style and you automatically tap into those styles when you encounter these different personalities. That's exactly how you should think about prompts. It's not that you need to memorize jargon or understand programming—you merely must adjust what you say and how you say it to get the most out of it, like you do with the people in your life.

This book will help you do just that.

For those who haven't read my book *AI Made Simple: A Beginner's Guide To Generative Intelligence*, 2nd Edition, the first two chapters of this book you are now reading will briefly present updated information on both generative AI as well as its most popular app, ChatGPT. (At the time of this writing, I am in the process of completing the third edition of *AI Made Simple*, which will most likely come out shortly after this book.) If you're already acquainted with these topics, then by all means feel free to skip ahead to chapter 3, where we'll dig into prompting.

Let's get started!

CHAPTER I

UNDERSTANDING AI AND CHATGPT

Before we get into prompts and prompting, I think it's important to define exactly what we mean by the term, "AI." AI refers to computer systems designed to perform tasks that typically require human intelligence, by simulating aspects of how we use our brains and attempting to replicate such intelligence and cognitive functions as:

1. Learning from experience
2. Understanding and responding to language
3. Recognizing patterns
4. Making decisions and solving problems
5. Adapting to new situations

These are tasks we learn to do through life experience—because we have to in order to survive. All these traits are crucial to navigating our messy lives. Technology, of course, doesn't have that life experience—all it needs is power to function. So, the challenge becomes how to effectively "teach" AI to do those five things. It's a challenge we haven't quite been able to meet yet, but the progress in the last few years has been breathtaking.

But let's go back to the beginnings of AI to understand its history and how it evolved. In the early 1950s, when the first computers were created, scientists had the idea they could aim for an elevated level of technological intelligence. The main obstacle to that achievement at the time was that computers were still primitive. They couldn't store information and could only execute commands one at a time, which meant they couldn't "remember" what they had done or learn from their actions.

Another problem? The expense. In the early 1950s, it could cost up to $200,000 a month to lease a computer—which were also huge and cumbersome. Only universities and big tech companies could afford to experiment with them. But engineers didn't give up on the AI dream.

The first step on the way to that dream was when the RAND Corporation funded the creation of Logic Theorist, a program designed to mimic human problem-solving skills. It was at this event in which this breakthrough was presented that the term "artificial intelligence" was first used. And it ignited the next two decades of AI research, aided by the rapid evolution of computers from 1957 to 1974. Computers became cheaper, smaller, more accessible, and with a lot more storage. However, they still weren't powerful enough to mimic human intelligence.

It wasn't until 1997 that the next huge leap came: Reigning world chess champion and grandmaster Gary Kasparov was defeated by IBM's Deep Blue, a chess-playing computer program, an event that shocked the world. In the same year, speech recognition software was implemented in the Windows operating system. Then, a few years later, Kismet, a robot that could recognize and display emotions, was developed. As the memory and processing capabilities of computers began doubling every year, a robust AI program was finally feasible, leading to 2022 and the public debut of generative AI and its most popular app to date, Open AI's ChatGPT, which, as of this moment, is currently the most widely used AI application, with more than 200 million weekly active users worldwide and growing.

The Foundation of AI

So how exactly does AI work? For the answer, it's useful to look at its primal building blocks, which scientists and engineers developed along the way (and which are still used to this day).

First, AI is underpinned by **NLP** (Natural Language Processing) which works through a set of algorithms that allow machines to process and analyze large chunks of language, and **LMs** (Language Models), which build an overarching architecture of language that the AI tool can use to interact with us as well as create materials from our prompts.

AI's development was then aided by the creation of **ML** (machine learning) in the 1980s. ML enabled computers and the like to actually *learn* from data. Inspired by the structure and function of the human brain, researchers developed artificial neural networks, which went beyond simply processing information to adapting that information based on experience.

Here's a simple explanation of what ML does: It learns from the information it's given. That makes it able to power such technology as image recognition programs, such as Google Lens. By telling it which images correspond to certain labels and categories it has been fed, the program can identify similar images and other relevant content. Likewise, when you see a list of movie recommendations on Netflix or any other streaming service, it's using ML to see what kind of shows you watched in the past and suggest ones that line up with your tastes. It's the same as when you buy something on Amazon and you are instantly provided with other product recommendations. It's a step down from the AI products currently being released, but it's still AI based in ML.

ML learns in a similar way as our brains do. For example, when a very young child first notices something as simple as a tree and asks a parent what it is, that parent tells the child that it's a tree and may explain that it's just a very, very large plant. From then on, whenever the child sees a tree, they know what they're looking at. Image recognition programs work similarly, and that tech is now used in countless complex real-world applications, such as security surveillance systems, medical imaging analysis, self-driving cars, and social media platforms, among others.

Which brings us to our last giant step forward, **generative AI.**

Generative AI is a huge evolution beyond traditional AI and ML. Prototype models first began popping up in the early 2000s, fueled by advancements in computing power, the availability of large datasets, and the development of deep learning computing techniques. These new models went beyond AI's old capabilities of classifying images, recognizing patterns, and making predictions based on those historic patterns. That was more of a reactive technology. Generative AI is much more proactive, as it can actually, when given direction with a few words (prompting), *produce* art, music, and text in the same way artists, musicians, and writers can.

While it won't deliver anything as artistically satisfying as, say, a Picasso painting or a Shakespearean sonnet (yet), generative AI can still produce works that appear incredibly professional and polished, if you know how to prompt it to do so (hence this book). Generative AI is already responsible for countless images circulating on the internet, as well as text-based works that range from simple short blog posts to poems to speeches to music lyrics to entire books, all written in different languages and utilizing the most current information available, depending on which AI assistant you're using.

This is very new. In the past, it was impressive to encounter an online AI-powered chatbot that would type out appropriate phrases to answer our questions. But anyone who has used this technology has also been disappointed by its limitations. Those old-school ML chatbots could answer simple questions and simple questions only—which is why most of us ended those kinds of frustrating time-consuming exchanges by asking to speak to a live agent. Generative AI breaks through those old limitations and is able to engage in complex conversations with humans.

The Training of Generative AI

As I said earlier, we have to teach AI how human intelligence works. We do that by feeding it as much information as possible. Generative AI models learn to represent the underlying structure and patterns of human works through a process called *training*. During training, these models are programmed with a large number of data samples—countless images, music, and/or text-based works—and they adjust their outputs accordingly.

Let's return to our tree example. A young child is told what a tree is and retains the memory of what one looks like so they can recognize one when they see it. That was as far as ML could take things as well. However, the child, if old enough, will also be capable of *drawing* a tree based on what they've learned and remembered about its appearance. That's how generative AI differs from ML—it too can create a picture of a tree based on other pictures of trees it "knows." With enough information in the prompt window, it can generate pictures of various kinds of trees: oak, pine, apple, or whatever is in its database.

But, as we've pointed out, generative AI can do far more than produce a simple image of a tree. It can be trained to read books on a subject and produce one of its own (and before you ask, no, I did not use generative AI to write this book!). It can also crawl the internet for current information on a news event and draft an article about it. It can do whatever its neural network enables it to do, depending on the breadth and depth of its training.

How is that different from musicians, artists, writers, performers, and the like who invariably say they were "inspired" by those that have come before them? You might say that the reality is that they were trained in those disciplines just as generative AI models are, and they learned how to produce similar works based on that knowledge. The problem comes when AI generates content that's too close to what it's been trained on. This has resulted in many copyright lawsuits, some of which have been dismissed, others of which have been moderately successful. Clearly, the courts will continue to grapple with the complexities introduced by AI technologies.

It's obvious that generative AI isn't just hype—it's the opening shot in a major revolution. This technology doesn't merely analyze data like traditional AI did; it creates content such as images, blog posts, code, podcasts, videos, music, and even entire books that didn't exist before. And that's an ability only we humans have had up until now.

Pulitzer Prize–winning *New York Times* columnist Thomas Friedman fully captured the dramatic impact of generative AI in his March 21, 2023, column, stating:

> This is a Promethean moment we've entered—one of those moments in history when certain new tools, ways of thinking or energy sources are introduced that are such a departure and advance on what existed before that you can't just change one thing, you have to change everything. That is, how you create, how you compete, how you collaborate, how you work, how you learn, how you govern and, yes, how you cheat, commit crimes and fight wars.[5]

---

5 https://www.nytimes.com/2023/03/21/opinion/artificial-intelligence-chatgpt.html

Generative AI Today

So, yes, generative AI has the ability to do a lot for us. And at this juncture, it may be hard for the average person to keep up with its progress as the AI landscape continues to change rapidly, thanks to the backing of hundreds of billions of dollars by investors anxious to get in on the next big thing.

Here are some key developments in the tech just since late 2022:

1. **Improved Language Models**
   - **GPT-4:** Released in March 2023, GPT-4 introduced greater accuracy, reasoning, and context understanding compared to GPT-3.5. The result? It can handle more complex instructions and deliver more nuanced outputs.
   - **Multimodal Models:** OpenAI expanded capabilities with models that process text, images, and audio, such as GPT-4o and other advancements in multimodal AI. The fact that you can now have a full two-way conversation with ChatGPT as a specific persona is pretty cool.
   - **Custom Instructions:** Users gained the ability to fine-tune how models respond, improving personalization and applicability.
   - **The GPT Store:** OpenAI's GPT Store offers custom GPTs— specialized versions of ChatGPT designed for specific tasks or industries, which include productivity tools, educational resources, creative writing aids, programming support, research and analysis, and image generation.
   - **Advanced Data Analysis:** ChatGPT (with the paid subscription) also allows you to upload a file that the GPT can then analyze, generate visualizations, or even execute code related to the data.

- **Apple Intelligence:** Apple Intelligence is a personal intelligence system that uses generative AI to help with writing, editing, image creation, and organization. It's available on iPhone 15 Pro, iPhone 15 Pro Max, and all iPhone 16 models running iOS 18.1 or later.

2. **AI-Driven Search and Knowledge Integration**

   - **Search Integration:** AI became integral to search engines, with OpenAI's ChatGPT incorporating web browsing capabilities. Microsoft and Google integrated generative AI into Bing and Google Search, respectively, transforming how users retrieve and process information.
   - **Knowledge Work Assistance:** Tools like Microsoft 365 Copilot and Google's Duet AI for Workspace introduced generative AI into productivity applications, automating tasks like drafting documents, creating presentations, and managing emails.

3. **Image and Video Generation**

   - **ChatGPT:** In early 2025, ChatGPT has integrated image creation directly in ChatGPT 4o, essentially minimizing its old platform called Dall-E.
   - **Midjourney and Stable Diffusion:** Competitors in image generation improved artistic control and user interaction for creating custom visuals.
   - **Runway:** Video generation tools like Runway enabled AI-driven video editing, background removal, and even generating video content from textual descriptions.
   - **Sora (by Open AI):** Want to create a video from scratch instantly? Sora could be your best bet. Released in December

2024, this AI app can create short video clips based on user prompts and can even extend existing short videos.

4. **Voice and Audio Applications**

- **ElevenLabs:** Pioneered realistic AI-generated voice synthesis for audiobooks, voiceovers, and real-time speech applications.
- **OpenAI's Voice and Image Features:** Introduced in ChatGPT, allows conversational voice interactions and image-based problem-solving.

5. **Specialized Applications**

- **Jasper and Copy.ai:** AI-powered writing assistants tailored for marketing and content creation.
- **Synthesia:** Facilitated video production using AI avatars, simplifying corporate training and marketing content creation.
- **Code Assistants:** GitHub Copilot and similar tools advanced in generating and debugging code, streamlining software development.

6. **Ethical and Legal Developments**

- As touched on earlier, growing debates on copyright and intellectual property led to lawsuits from artists, writers, and content creators. Some cases, such as those involving AI image generators and training data, have set early precedents, but it's clear that additional laws and regulations may be necessary.

7. **Autonomous AI Agents**

- Companies began exploring AI agents capable of operating independently to perform tasks with minimal human intervention—and in the next 2–3 years they will be everywhere. OpenAI's plans for "Operator" reflect this trend. Let's just hope this doesn't lead to Hal 9000, from the movie *2001*.

8. **AI Democratization**

- Platforms like OpenAI's API and open-source models like Llama 2 from Meta made generative AI more accessible to developers and businesses, fostering innovation across industries.

9. **Challenges and Controversies**

- Issues like AI bias, hallucinations, and ethical concerns about job displacement and misinformation remain key focus areas, although AI engineers continue to try to mitigate these problematic areas. AI hallucinations are responses that the technology gives that are inaccurate, unfounded, or—frighteningly—entirely fabricated while presenting them as if they're facts. For example, if you asked ChatGPT who invented a time machine, it could conceivably answer "Dr. Emmett Brown," based on Christopher Lloyd's character in the popular *Back to the Future* film trilogy. This is why it is important to double-check responses; AI is not an all-knowing flawless entity of knowledge—so always double check your outputs!

- "Deepfakes" continue to plague us on social media and elsewhere. These are a type of synthetic media created using AI tools in order to manipulate or generate visual and audio content to create highly realistic but fabricated representations of individuals. These deceptions could make you believe in ridiculous lies, like Tom Cruise shilling for nutritional supplements or Taylor Swift advocating for someone she never would in real life. They generally get called out quickly, but they can still do a great deal of damage. Businesses, families, and individuals are all at risk when deepfakes are used for scams and smears, so be vigilant.

Big picture? The main trend in generative AI has been a transition from the initial releases of experimental standalone tools to the tech being integrated into homes, businesses, stores, and . . . well, everything (see the introduction to this book for more examples). However, the standalone tools are still very popular; the following is a list of some of the more popular ones at the time of publication.

AI Generators

Chat GPT Image Generator

Also from OpenAI, ChatGPT can now generate detailed images from textual descriptions, enabling users to create visuals by simply describing them in words.

Midjourney

An independent research lab, Midjourney offers an AI program (primarily accessed via the Discord platform) that creates images from textual descriptions, focusing on artistic and imaginative visuals.

Jasper

Jasper is an AI writing assistant designed for marketers, bloggers, and content creators, helping generate content ideas, drafts, and marketing copy.

GitHub Copilot

A collaboration between GitHub and OpenAI, Copilot assists developers by suggesting code snippets and functions as they write, streamlining the coding process. GitHub is also responsible for the Copilot add-ons available on Windows and other Microsoft products.

Adobe Firefly

Adobe's generative AI suite, Firefly, focuses on generating images and text effects, integrating seamlessly with Adobe's creative tools.

Runway

Runway offers AI-powered tools for video editing, including background removal, motion tracking, and video generation from text prompts.

ElevenLabs

Specializing in AI voice synthesis, ElevenLabs provides tools for generating natural-sounding speech, useful in audiobooks, voiceovers, and more.

Synthesia

Synthesia enables users to create videos with AI-generated avatars speaking in multiple languages, streamlining corporate training and marketing content production.

Wix ADI (Artificial Design Intelligence)

Wix's ADI helps users build personalized websites by leveraging AI to design layouts and suggest content based on user preferences.

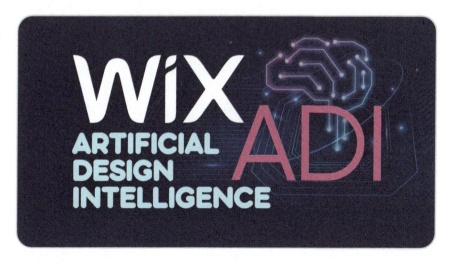

If you've noticed something missing from the above list, you're not wrong—I've purposely saved ChatGPT, the most popular of the generative AI chatbots, for its own chapter. In terms of learning how to use prompts effectively, ChatGPT is the best place to learn how to use prompts correctly, so it's important you understand what the AI assistant is all about. I'll help you tackle that challenge in the next chapter. And by the way, if you want a more detailed look at the evolution of generative AI as well as its many applications, you might want to check out my previous best-selling book, *AI Made Simple*, 2nd Edition.

CHAPTER 2

THE ABCS OF CHATGPT

The big AI game changer of 2022, ChatGPT was one of the first fully functional AI assistants to be released for public use and was the most impactful and widely recognized. Since this is the most popular AI Assistant, and the one most of you will be using, we're going to spend this chapter talking about its roots, its abilities, and its limitations, so you can gain a deeper understanding of the technology.

The Birth of ChatGPT

Even though ChatGPT was released in 2022, it had been in development for a few years prior to that. OpenAI began working on it in 2017, with the aim of creating a series of generative AI models designed to understand and produce human-like text. This was only possible because of the creation of transformer architecture, introduced in a seminal 2017 Google research paper titled "Attention Is All You Need." The transformer model was a game changer and became foundational in modern AI, serving as the basis for LLMs like GPT.

The main difference was that earlier AI models were programmed to read each word in a sentence individually without much of a clue as to how they related to each other. If you wrote a sentence that said, "The police pursued the criminal," AI models really wouldn't understand the idea of what you were saying. With the transformer, however, suddenly, the model was able to understand how words in a sentence *related* to each other. With the sample sentence we just used, the transformer model would understand that the police were the ones in pursuit of the criminal. Seems simple to us, right? Well, not so simple for a piece of cold technology!

The way the transformer grasps how words relate to each other is through a tactic called "attention." The transformer knows to pay more attention to the important parts of the sentence, such as the main nouns and verbs. From there, it stacks multiple layers of attention and processing, with each layer refining the model's understanding of the text the user inputs. You might want to think of it like peeling an onion—with each layer, the model "gets" more of what you're telling it. And because the transformer model also doesn't have to read text in a specific order like the older models, it's faster and is better able to comprehend what you write.

With this breakthrough idea, it didn't take long to create ChatGPT, with the first iteration completed in 2018, followed by ChatGPT-2 in 2019. There, it stalled for a while, due to concerns about how the tech could be misused, a debate that still goes on to this day. Finally, in 2020, ChatGPT-3 was released, a significantly scaled-up model from the 2.0 version, allowing for more nuanced and context-aware text generation. It also had more extensive training through diverse datasets sourced from the internet, including books, websites, and other publicly available texts, to learn language patterns and knowledge.

When ChatGPT-3.5 was finally made available to all of us in late 2022, the engineers had fine-tuned it, so it was built for more conversational and interactive tasks that were more user-friendly. Human trainers were used to simulate conversations and rate ChatGPT's responses to teach the model how to generate helpful, accurate, and safe outputs. For the latest version, ChatGPT-4 (released in 2023) was equipped with increased reasoning, and accuracy capabilities, along with added multimodal capabilities (e.g., processing images and audio).

To this day, ChatGPT continues to be improved, aided by continuous feedback from users and testers that helps the engineers identify weaknesses and provides focus for fixes. Currently, it's not only available as a standalone tool on browsers and phone apps, but also licensed to other products, such as Microsoft's Copilot and Bing, and used in other industries such as education, customer service, and software development.

What ChatGPT Can and Can't Do

As you can see, ChatGPT is the result of years of research in AI and the successful leveraging of innovative technologies and iterative refinement, and is now capable of creating meaningful and coherent conversations. And you can access what's called ChatGPT-4 mini for free. The mini differs from the full version by not being able to handle complex tasks as well as the full version and occasionally producing less precise answers. Because it's a smaller and more compact version, however, it's faster than the full version and is perfect for most routine requests.

However, if you want access to the full version—or, better yet, ChatGPT-4.0 Turbo, a more efficient and faster version of the full version—it will cost you. OpenAI provides access through a subscription plan that currently charges $20 a month for an individual user or if you want to get this for your company, I recommend getting the $25 a month Team version, this version allows you to opt out of using your data for training. (ChatGPT has an advanced $200/month option as well, but that may be overkill for you at this time). That includes

ChatGPT-4's image-creation capabilities. For example, I just asked it to generate an image of a bluebird in an elm tree. It instantly came up with this:

What else can you do with ChatGPT-4? Well, I went straight to the source and asked it what it can do. Here's its reply:

General Language Processing

- **Text Understanding**: Comprehends complex questions, instructions, and nuanced prompts.
- **Text Generation**: Creates detailed, coherent, and contextually appropriate responses in various tones and styles.

- **Multilingual Support**: Understands and generates content in multiple languages.
- **Context Awareness**: Maintains context over extended conversations, allowing for more coherent and logical exchanges.

Creative Writing

- **Storytelling**: Crafts engaging stories, poems, or scripts tailored to specific prompts.
- **Editing and Polishing**: Refines text for grammar, tone, clarity, and style.
- **Ideation**: Generates ideas for novels, essays, or creative projects.

Educational Assistance

- **Explaining Concepts**: Breaks down complex topics into understandable explanations.
- **Problem-Solving**: Solves math problems, explains processes, or provides step-by-step instructions.
- **Tutoring**: Offers tailored guidance on a variety of subjects.

Professional Applications

- **Business Writing**: Creates reports, proposals, emails, or marketing copy.
- **Sales Support**: Assists with pitches, cold outreach, or crafting sales materials.
- **Resumes & Cover Letters**: Reviews and creates polished resumes and cover letters.
- **Code Assistance**: Writes, reviews, and debugs code in multiple programming languages.

Technical Skills

- **Code Generation**: Creates scripts and applications in languages like Python, JavaScript, SQL, and more.
- **Data Analysis**: Provides insights into data trends, writes code for analysis, or interprets data-related queries.
- **Tool Integration**: Works with tools for visualization, such as matplotlib, pandas, or other Python libraries.

Creative and Visual Assistance

- **Image Descriptions**: Describes or generates text-based prompts for artistic or technical visualization.
- **ChatGPT Image**: Generates detailed image descriptions to create AI-generated visuals.

Research and Knowledge

- **Fact-Based Responses**: Provides factual and up-to-date information (with some limitations on real-time updates unless web tools are utilized).
- **Comparative Analysis**: Helps compare ideas, tools, or concepts side-by-side.
- **Web Integration**: Uses live web search tools to retrieve current and location-specific information.

Personal Assistance

- **Scheduling and Planning**: Assists in creating plans, itineraries, or schedules.
- **Advice and Counseling**: Provides non-legal, non-medical advice or emotional support.

- **Customized Responses**: Tailors outputs to fit personal styles or specific needs.

Analytical and Logical Tasks

- **Problem Solving**: Tackles puzzles, riddles, or logical problems.
- **Data Interpretation**: Analyzes trends, charts, or raw data for insights.

Customization and Formatting

- **Style Adaptation**: Mimics formal, casual, persuasive, or technical tones.
- **Format Expertise**: Converts content into specific formats, such as markdown, LaTeX, or HTML.
- **Document Preparation**: Creates documents, presentations, or structured outlines.

Interactive Features

- **Chat Personalization**: Adapts to user preferences, such as tone or complexity, over time.
- **Memory (Optional)**: Can retain contextual memory during conversations for improved interactions.

That's a lot—but far from everything ChatGPT will be able to do in the future. As a matter of fact, right now it's on the cusp of a huge breakthrough with a new feature that will allow it to access the contents of your apps on the macOS, a feature already available for Mac users. This new feature, available in a desktop app, is designed to make it easier to get the AI app's input on what you're doing in another app without having to take a screenshot or copy and paste text. The app also contains Advanced Voice, which gives you the ability to have a "conversation" with ChatGPT as if it were a human![6]

Everything, however, has a downside, so to be fair, we should also understand the limitations of ChatGPT. It may be advanced tech, but it has weaknesses all users should be very wary of, including the following.

- **Lack of Personal Experience/Emotions**

  If you're a fan of the superhero, The Vision, or, to go back further, Mr. Spock from *Star Trek*, you know that those characters don't experience the same level of emotions as the rest of us do—but they at least have some insight into them. ChatGPT does not. It can simulate emotions based on data it's been trained on, but because it doesn't "live" in the way you and I do, it can't really understand them. Obviously, it also lacks the ability to form personal relationships, so if you think ChatGPT is crushing on you, it's time to get out more!

- **Ethical and Safety Constraints**

  OpenAI is doing everything it can to put in place guardrails that will prevent it from doing harm to users. It will not provide harmful, unethical, or unsafe advice nor will it engage in conversations that encourage illegal activity, harmful behavior, or violence.

- **Language Limitations**

  ChatGPT works best in languages it's been trained on (primarily English). It can handle a few other languages proficiently as well and this is another area where improvement will continue.

---

6   https://www.tomsguide.com/ai/chatgpt/chatgpt-will-soon-be-able-to-see-your-mac-apps-and-provide-real-time-advice-this-is-huge

You can actually have a two-way conversation in Chinese—just specify if you want to have it in Mandarin, Cantonese, or Simplified Chinese, and that you want it to be conversational, not formal.

- **Occasional Inaccuracies**

  Although ChatGPT is becoming more and more accurate, it can still sometimes get facts wrong, especially if its training data includes incorrect or outdated information. This is why you should always fact-check critical details it provides, just to make sure. The good news is that ChatGPT advanced models can now surf the web and show you the sources it's pulling its information from.

- **Creativity Has Boundaries**

  Yes, ChatGPT can create stories, ideas, and visuals—but its creativity is very derivative, because it's building on patterns in existing data. True innovation is beyond it, so we humans still hold that advantage.

So, those are the main areas where ChatGPT might fail you. Keep those top of mind as you work with it so you can avoid any issues with its output.

Most of ChatGPT's problems arise simply because the dataset that underpins it comes primarily from the internet, which, as you might have experienced for yourself, sometimes passes off misinformation or opinion as truth. In other words, ChatGPT's biggest problem is that it's a reflection of us—and human nature. So, it encounters the same prejudices and propaganda that we all do when we go online to certain sites or social media accounts. Depending on what you're asking ChatGPT to do, you must be aware of these limitations. If you're asking for ideas for a kid's birthday party, this won't be that big a concern. But if you ask a charged political question, the result could be skewed or not to your liking. This kind of distorted outcome is becoming much rarer, but be wary, as its technology sometimes can't separate fact from fiction.

Getting Started

When you navigate your browser to the ChatGPT home page (https://chatgpt.com/), this is what you'll see (as of the writing of this book; you can also use the simpler chat.com):

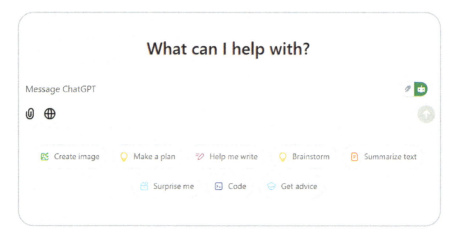

Right below the question, "What can I help with?" you'll see the shaded area meant for your typed prompt, along with a couple of other icons. If you click on the globe icon, you can search the web, while the paper clip icon to the left of it is for attaching files, files you might want ChatGPT to analyze, summarize, or merely learn from the information they contain.

Below is a screenshot of what you'll find if you're already subscribing to the latest version of ChatGPT (called 4o). The + symbol is where you can attach a file, the globe icon is what you use for search, the telescope is for using the Deep Research feature (use this feature if you want PhD level support). The other additional icons, are a microphone feature where you can record your prompts to ChatGPT, and the black circular one all the way to the right, puts you in audio mode, where you can have a direct conversation with ChatGPT. Simply talk to it, and tell it what you need directly to the app and receive audible responses in return. My advice, if you want to have a conversation with ChatGPT, use the mobile APP, it's easier to use.

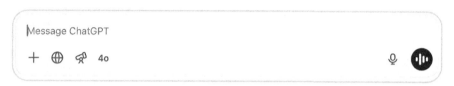

Underneath that, you'll find several options for a few of the more popular tasks that ChatGPT can perform for you. Most are pretty self-explanatory, but I do recommend the "Surprise me" task if you really want to have some fun. Here's the pulldown menu that appears when you click on it in the free ChatGPT version:

Well, I went ahead and chose "Surprise me with a fact from the *Farmer's Almanac.*"

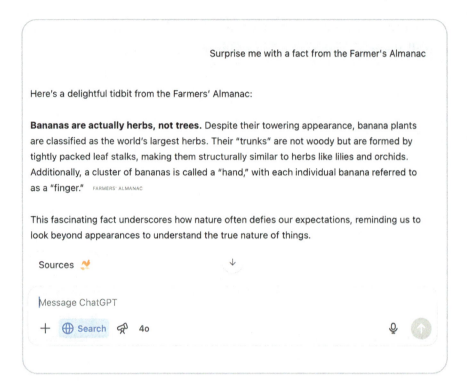

As you can see not only did it search the web, it provided me with the link to the actual source. Simply click on the source and you can see where it pulled its information from. It is surprisingly easy to use—all you have to do is type in a prompt (a question or request) and it will immediately respond. For example, I asked it a fairly straightforward question—"What is ChatGPT?"—and its answer is below:

ChatGPT is an advanced AI language model developed by OpenAI, designed to generate human-like text based on user input. It excels in tasks such as drafting emails, writing essays, and providing code assistance. OPENAI

Initially released in November 2022, ChatGPT has undergone significant enhancements. The latest iteration, GPT-4o, introduces features like voice interaction and image recognition, enabling users to engage in natural conversations and interpret visual inputs. THE SUN

ChatGPT is accessible through various platforms, including web browsers and dedicated applications for iOS and macOS. It offers both free and subscription-based plans, with premium tiers providing access to advanced functionalities and increased usage limits. OPENAI

The model has been integrated into numerous applications, such as Microsoft's Copilot, enhancing productivity tools by offering AI-driven assistance. FAST COMPANY

While ChatGPT is a powerful tool, it's important to note that it may occasionally produce inaccurate or nonsensical responses. Users are advised to verify critical information and use the model as a supplementary aid rather than a sole source of truth. OPENAI HELP

Sources

A couple things to note. First, you'll see ChatGPT lists sources for its facts after every paragraph. This is a significant improvement over previous versions, where frequently it would not provide where it obtained its information.

You'll also notice under the prompt box another series of small icons. If you click on the first one, ChatGPT will "read" your answer out loud (just remember to turn up your sound). Click on the second icon and you can continue the interaction on the subject matter you're discussing. The third and fourth icons are your standard "like" and "dislike" icons, so you can give direct feedback about ChatGPT's answers. The last icon lets you change the ChatGPT model you're working with.

Now that you know the basics of ChatGPT, we can finally move on to the subject of this book, which is how to use prompts most effectively. We'll do that in the very next chapter.

CHAPTER 3

PROMPTING 101

Imagine you're a server at a restaurant. You ask a diner, sitting by himself, what he wants to eat. This guy simply says, "Get me soup."

You respond, "What kind of soup? We have . . . "

"Just soup!" he snaps, indicating the conversation is over. You shrug, go back to the kitchen and eventually emerge with a bowl of tomato soup, which you place in front of him on the table.

The diner looks at it enraged.

"No! No, no, no! I wanted chicken noodle! With crackers!"

Well, of course, the diner never said any of that. And yet he's shocked you didn't deliver exactly what he wanted.

Within that anecdote is probably the most important truth to remember when using prompts in ChatGPT or any AI device: The more details you provide, the closer generative AI can come to delivering what you want.

As a server, you couldn't read the mind of our soup-obsessed diner, so you couldn't know precisely what he wanted. Well, ChatGPT can't read your mind either (although, within a few years, who knows?). Of course, as you'll see, you can keep directing ChatGPT to change its responses as you get more specific, but my point is you can't take for granted things that you might if you were talking to a real live flesh-and-blood person. ChatGPT lacks life experience and can take your words much too literally. Which reminds me of a character in the original version of *The Manchurian Candidate* who's been brainwashed to do exactly what he's instructed. And I mean *exactly*. So, when someone gets irritated with him and tells him to "Go jump in the lake," he calmly leaves, gets in his car, drives all the way to a lake, calmly gets out of the car, and strolls over to it, where he. . . jumps in the lake.

So, effectively using prompts isn't quite as easy as you might think, although engineers continue to improve AI's interface. And even though generative AI is based on how we communicate, it's still not human and you can't treat it like it is, at least not yet (but it can't hurt to be polite as mentioned earlier). Instead, you have to tell it what you want in a way that it will understand, and the way you do that is through prompts.

In this chapter, I'll walk you through the basics of prompting and show you some real-life examples of how it works. This will give you an idea of how it works and the kinds of results you can expect based on the prompts you give ChatGPT. At the end of the book, I've also included a basic prompt library to help you get started. Let me quickly add that you don't have to be a computer programmer or fully understand the technology to use ChatGPT effectively. Yes, there is definitely a science behind it, but there's also an art in terms of how you communicate with AI. The more prompting you do with ChatGPT, the higher your comfort factor will be. If it helps, pretend you're talking to another person instead of an AI app. It's been designed to replicate human interactions and while that element hasn't been perfected yet, you'll see it's close enough to successfully "talk" to it. To master prompting you need to become a storyteller, so the more you can give ChatGPT to work with, the better the output will be. Over time, this will be an absolute requirement in all aspects of what we do. It's also why Prompt Engineering as a job is exploding, with salaries already reaching the high six and low seven figures.

First Steps

Let's start by defining what a prompt is. Simply put, a prompt refers to whatever command you enter into ChatGPT's text box (or the text box of any generative AI tool) to elicit the information or generate the content you're after. Even if you haven't used ChatGPT before, you probably already have experience using prompts if you've used online automated chatbots in the past. However, those that were in operation prior to the release of generative AI were much more rudimentary and very frustrating. They couldn't respond to specifics they hadn't been programmed with, so they were very limited in their responses. If you were like most people, you quickly asked for a live agent to get the answers you were after.

Well, as we shared in the last chapter, ChatGPT is much more responsive and capable than they were. If you were to compare the two, you could say that the old chatbot is akin to a horse and buggy, while ChatGPT is more like a sleek Lamborghini. It can take you for an amazing ride—*if* you know how to get the most out of it, which is what I'll help you do with the information in this book.

First, I'm going to assume you're more than capable of typing in a short question as a prompt to get a short answer, whether it's a math problem, translating something from or into a different language, or wanting to know a simple fact, like the capital of New Hampshire or when World War II started. That's pretty straightforward, almost as simple as Googling those kinds of easy queries. That's why, in this book, we're going to focus on using ChatGPT to do more complex—as well as more creative—tasks.

The first step in preparing ChatGPT to do that type of task is to clear any previous conversations you might have had with the bot by starting a new conversation. That way, it's not influenced by anything you've written that doesn't pertain to the job at hand. So, start with a fresh slate—or in this case, a new prompt. You can do this by clicking on the "New Chat" icon at the top left of the ChatGPT browser page (you need to have the sidebar open to see it).[7]

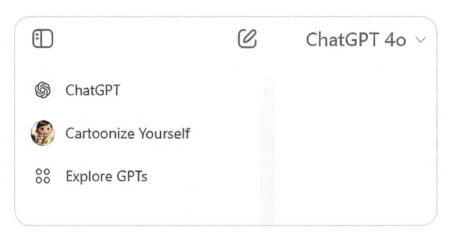

Above, you see a screenshot of the top left corner of the ChatGPT browser interface. The little icon between the text "ChatGPT 4o" and the sidebar icon is the "New Chat" icon. If you're using the ChatGPT app, which is available on most operating systems and is very easy to use, the "New Chat" Icon is at the top right corner, as you can see in the screenshot below.

---

7   Just to let you know, I'm going to be referring to the paid version of the app, which requires a monthly $20 subscription—the free version works quite well but doesn't have all the features I'm going to be discussing.

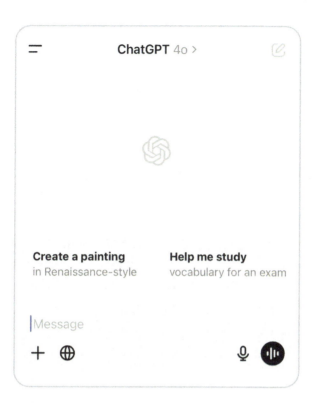

Once you've cleared the chat field, it's time to start your session. If you just have a simple question to ask, hopefully more complex than "Who's buried in Grant's Tomb?," go ahead and ask it.

(By the way, ChatGPT knows what you're up to with that question. . .)

 The answer to the riddle "Who is buried in Grant's Tomb?" is Ulysses S. Grant and his wife, Julia Dent Grant.

This is often used as a trick question because it seems to imply there's a twist, but it's straightforward—Grant and his wife are indeed entombed there.

However, if you're doing something a little more complicated, you might want to "introduce" yourself to ChatGPT by telling it a little bit about yourself in a couple of sentences so it knows who you are and can use that information to help elicit more helpful answers. For example, if you're a consumer blogger who specializes in shopping on a budget, tell the AI tool that. Or, if you're planning a child's birthday party, tell it a little about the child and their likes and dislikes. The more background information you provide to ChatGPT, the more specific and targeted its response will be.

To be clear, if you're just asking something simple, you really don't have to introduce yourself. But, when people get bad results from a ChatGPT request, it's often because they're feeding it short, poorly written prompts and expecting the technology to magically "get" what they're after. While ChatGPT-4 does have a memory function and will start to "know" you much as an acquaintance would, you still may need to fill in some blanks. (Incidentally, to enable the memory feature, go to ChatGPT settings, select Personalization, and turn on the Memory setting.) Remember: Generative AI *can't* read your mind. On average, a single good-to-great prompt can be anywhere from 100 to 400 words, so don't limit yourself. The mistake that people new to prompting make is that they treat the prompt box as a search engine and type in a simple short prompt. ChatGPT isn't a Google web search, so don't treat it that way. Be as complicated as you want and don't be afraid to keep prompting to achieve the results you're after.

For example, let's say I use this as a prompt:

> *"Write a cover letter for a job application."*

Here's what ChatGPT will spit out:

Dear [Hiring Manager's Name],

I am writing to express my interest in the [Position Title] role at [Company Name]. With a strong background in [your field or industry] and a proven track record of [specific relevant skills or achievements], I am confident in my ability to contribute positively to your team.

Throughout my career, I have consistently demonstrated strengths in [list 2–3 core skills relevant to the job]. I take pride in my ability to [mention a key capability or accomplishment, such as solving problems, improving processes, or driving results]. These experiences have equipped me with the expertise to excel in fast-paced, dynamic environments like yours.

What excites me most about this opportunity is [mention something specific about the company or role that resonates with you, such as their mission, culture, or a recent achievement]. I am eager to bring my [specific qualities or experiences] to support the organization's continued success and growth.

I would welcome the chance to discuss how my skills and experiences align with your needs. Thank you for considering my application, and I look forward to the possibility of contributing to the success of your team.

Sincerely,

[Your Name]

Because I told ChatGPT nothing about me, all it can do is "write" what closely resembles a generic cover letter template, which I could have easily found online to modify for my own needs. This is a waste of ChatGPT's talents, to be blunt. It's also a waste of my time to have to make all those modifications myself—so why not give ChatGPT the details it needs to make the letter more specific? That way, it can do the work itself, and I don't have to. Keeping that in mind, I will put in a more targeted prompt:

> *I am a salesperson with 10 years of experience who is the top salesperson at my company. I have an MBA from Harvard and have won multiple awards as "Salesperson of the Month" for revenue I've generated. I know how to sell better than anyone I know. The company I am applying to is the number one car retailer in southern Nebraska and it is for the sales manager position. Write me a cover letter for a job application.*

Here's what ChatGPT came up with:

Dear [Hiring Manager's Name],

I am excited to apply for the Sales Manager position at [Company Name]. With over a decade of proven sales expertise, an MBA from Harvard, and a track record as the top salesperson at my current company, I am confident in my ability to drive revenue growth, mentor high-performing teams, and contribute to [Company Name]'s continued success as the number one car retailer in southern Nebraska.

Throughout my career, I have consistently exceeded sales targets, earning multiple "Salesperson of the

Month" awards for record-breaking revenue. I have built my success on a deep understanding of customer psychology, data-driven sales strategies, and a relentless commitment to delivering results. Beyond individual performance, I thrive in leadership roles—coaching teams to elevate their skills, improve closing rates, and foster lasting customer relationships that drive repeat business.

[Company Name]'s reputation for excellence aligns perfectly with my drive to lead high-performing teams and implement innovative sales strategies. I would welcome the opportunity to discuss how my expertise can contribute to your continued market dominance. Please feel free to contact me at your convenience to schedule a conversation.

Thank you for your time and consideration. I look forward to the possibility of joining your team.

Best regards,

[Your Name]

Just so you know, I made up all those personal details. I have never applied for a position in southern Nebraska, and I got my MBA at USC, not Harvard. But the important thing is that you can see how more detail helps ChatGPT get closer to the mark—which, in this case, is a more personalized and usable output. And you don't have to stop there. You can give more details and even ask ChatGPT to change the tone of the letter if you want. Or change the length of the letter. Below, you'll see what happened when I asked ChatGPT to be more casual and also to shorten the letter by 75 words (along with a final editorial comment by ChatGPT as to what it believes it accomplished with this new version).

Dear [Hiring Manager's Name],

I'm excited to apply for the Sales Manager position at [Company Name]. With 10 years of experience and a track record as the top salesperson at my current company, I'm confident I can contribute to your team's success.

I've consistently exceeded revenue goals, earning multiple "Salesperson of the Month" awards. My Harvard MBA equips me with strategic leadership skills, and I'm passionate about building strong teams and driving results.

[Company Name]'s reputation as the top car retailer in southern Nebraska aligns with my expertise and goals. I'd love the chance to discuss how my experience can benefit your team.

Thank you for considering my application, and I look forward to connecting soon.

Best regards,

[Your Name]

This version trims unnecessary repetition while keeping your key strengths front and center.

I could easily keep going, requesting changes until it creates what I believe to be the perfect cover letter for my purposes. When you continue to finesse ChatGPT (or any generative AI application) through a sequence of prompts, each designed to help it produce exactly what you want, it's known as "prompt chaining," which we'll talk about in the next chapter.

Another helpful and basic tip for prompting is to assign ChatGPT a **persona**. You assign it a personality or role through a prompt or series of prompts by being as detailed as you can be. ChatGPT will do its best to bring that persona to "life." The advantage of this technique is that when you do create a persona for the app, it will be better able to tailor its responses, advice, and solutions to align with your specific needs, preferences, and goals. For example, let's say you're a very experienced salesperson, but you still want to continue to improve. If you ask ChatGPT for sales tips, you'll likely only get the most basic advice. However, if you ask it to assume the role of an expert salesperson talking to other expert salespeople, you'll get the more advanced strategies you're after. Personas help you filter out irrelevant information and ensure the advice is directly applicable to your situation. At the same time, the more you tell ChatGPT about your persona, that is, who you are and what you want from the app, the more targeted its responses will be.

Using personas also helps enhance ChatGPT's creativity, because it can spark ideas that are aligned with your mindset. For example, let's say our expert salesperson is looking for high-risk/high-reward strategies. If you let the app know that, it will gravitate to those types of approaches.

By assigning ChatGPT a persona—and sharing your own— you're equipping the AI app with the context it needs to address your specific requests in the way you want them addressed. It makes your collaboration with ChatGPT smoother, more efficient, and more productive.

For example, you can use ChatGPT to help you brainstorm a business idea just by giving it the persona of a successful entrepreneur. That kind of prompt could go like this:

> *Hi ChatGPT, I need help brainstorming my new business idea. Pretend you're Mark Cuban and give me advice on how best to get my startup launched, scaled, and then provide step-by-step instructions to get on Shark Tank.*

You can use a multitude of personas. For example, maybe you want to give a classy, but funny toast at a wedding. You could try asking ChatGPT to help you by taking on the persona of President Obama. Want to win next summer's chili cookoff? Ask ChatGPT to take on the persona of Food Network celebrity chef Bobby Flay and provide the recipe for the world's best chili. You can literally ask ChatGPT to be anyone in the past or present, real or fictional, and then have a two-way conversation with the persona you specified. Try it!

Rules of the Road for Prompts

To close out this chapter, let me share some overall pointers on how to create the kinds of prompts that will direct ChatGPT to deliver what you're after:

- **Be specific and clear.** Provide ChatGPT with as much detailed and targeted language as necessary, so it understands exactly what you want. The more complex the ask, the more detail you should provide through your initial description of the task or through the process of prompt chaining.
- **Provide context.** As seen with the job cover letter, the more context and background information you provide, the better

ChatGPT can tailor its response to your requirements. You can even upload documents and other specific information that may not have been available to ChatGPT through its previous training.

- **Avoid bias.** Instruct ChatGPT to "ensure your answer is unbiased and does not rely on stereotypes," if you think this may be an issue. Independently vet anything that you feel is questionable.

- **Don't be afraid to rephrase.** Not satisfied with how the ChatGPT is responding? Reword your query or ask it in a different way. Slight changes in phrasing can sometimes lead to significantly different results.

- **Set constraints and format.** Do you want ChatGPT to write you a LinkedIn post? A blog post? A press release? Make sure you let it know the format in which you want your content and then give it guidelines, such as how long you want it to be, the tone of the writing (casual, formal, etc.), and so forth. You can even provide examples of how you want the final product to read. State any other requirements you need fulfilled, such as keywords, regulations, or other instructions.

- **Give ChatGPT a voice.** One of the things you can do is to tell ChatGPT to provide results using a "voice" or specific style. For example, you can ask it to write in the style of anyone from Ernest Hemingway to Kara Swisher (if you don't know who she is, look her up—she's great!). You can also tell ChatGPT to pretend it's the greatest chef in the world and you want it to create a seven-course dinner using a fusion of Indian and Chinese food. Looking for help creating a business launch plan for your new start-up? Then tell ChatGPT to assume it's a successful entrepreneur like Mark Cuban and you want it to create a ten-step launch plan for success. You can do this type of prompting in the voice of any prominent public figure in any occupation. Or try asking ChatGPT to write a toast for a best man to give at a wedding in the voice of President Obama or Howard Stern—and it will do it! Ask for a specific tone for the content you want and ChatGPT will do its best to provide it.

- **Provide a structure for it to follow.** For example, if you're asking it to write a blog post, give it a step-by-step outline, such as, (1) start with an attention-getting statement, (2) set up the problem, (3) resolve the problem, and (4) finish by providing value. Do this through an 800-word blog post at a fifth-grade reading level in the first person." Then input the information you want in the blog.

- Finally, **there's no need to be polite** when addressing ChatGPT. It doesn't need the niceties of "please," "thank you," or even "I would like you to." It doesn't care. It just wants to be told what to do (unlike most of the people I know). And it has no feelings to hurt if you're abrupt with it. It's not human—you can impose on it all you want! *However*, being nice to it doesn't hurt and in fact may help you mentally get over the fact that you are talking to an algorithm. Plus, if you are indeed afraid that the AI overlords will eventually come for us all, then go ahead and be nice—its programming may hopefully remember you fondly after the revolution is complete.

Your most important takeaways about prompts should be that **clarity and specificity are key**. A well-crafted prompt guides the AI to provide the most accurate, relevant, and helpful response. A good way to guide your promptings is by keeping in mind the acronym **RTCA, which stands for "Role, Task, Context, Ask."** First, you assign ChatGPT a **role**; then you introduce a **task** for it to perform, explaining any **context** that may be important; and finally, you **ask** it to obey the criteria you want it to use.

Here's a prompt that's a perfect example of putting RTCA to work:

> *Act like you're an expert travel agent that specializes in African safaris. Come up with a 10-day itinerary for me and my family that takes us to the Serengeti and the Silverback Gorillas in Rwanda. We would like to stay in four-star level resorts that have activities for kids. Please note that my daughter is lactose intolerant and I am a vegetarian. We really want to make amazing family memories and get as close as possible to the wildlife. We will be flying from Los Angeles on Feb 20th, 2025.*

The "role" I asked ChatGPT to assume was that of an expert travel agent. The "task" I wanted performed was to produce an itinerary for an African safari. The "context" was all my parameters—dates, specific requests, and what I wanted the general spirit of the trip to be, and the "ask" was for it to obey the criteria I outlined (producing the itinerary). As follows is ChatGPT's lengthy response:

Here's a detailed 10-day African Safari itinerary for your family, starting with your flight from Los Angeles on February 20, 2025:

Day 1: February 20, 2025 - Travel

Depart Los Angeles (LAX) on an overnight flight to Kilimanjaro International Airport, Tanzania, with a connecting flight in a major international hub.

Day 2: February 21, 2025 - Arrival in Tanzania

Morning: Arrive at Kilimanjaro International Airport. A guide will meet you for a short transfer to your hotel in Arusha.

Accommodation: Four-star lodge in Arusha with a pool and kids' play area (e.g., Arusha Coffee Lodge).

Meals: Vegetarian and lactose-free options pre-arranged.

Activity: Relax after your flight; enjoy the lodge's gardens and family-friendly amenities.

Day 3: February 22, 2025 - Serengeti National Park

Morning: Take a short domestic flight to the Serengeti.

Accommodation: Four-star family tented camp (e.g., Serengeti Serena Safari Lodge) with stunning views and kids' activities like guided nature walks.

Activity: Afternoon game drive to spot elephants, giraffes, and lions.

Meals: Lodge caters to dietary needs.

Day 4: February 23, 2025 - Full Day in the Serengeti

Morning: Sunrise hot air balloon safari (optional for older kids and adults).

Day: Full-day game drive with a picnic lunch to explore more of the Serengeti's wildlife, including wildebeest, zebras, and cheetahs.

Evening: Storytime around the campfire for kids while adults relax with scenic views.

Day 5: February 24, 2025 - Ngorongoro Crater

Morning: Drive to the Ngorongoro Conservation Area.

Accommodation: Four-star lodge overlooking the crater (e.g., Ngorongoro Serena Safari Lodge).

Activity: Afternoon game drive in the crater, renowned for its dense wildlife.

Meals: Freshly prepared meals catering to your family's dietary preferences.

Day 6: February 25, 2025 - Travel to Rwanda

Morning: Return to Arusha for a short flight to Kigali, Rwanda.

Accommodation: Four-star Kigali hotel (e.g., Kigali Serena Hotel).

Activity: Visit the Kigali Genocide Memorial (optional and age-appropriate).

Evening: Relax and prepare for the gorilla trek.

Day 7: February 26, 2025 - Volcanoes National Park

Morning: Transfer to Volcanoes National Park.

Accommodation: Family-friendly lodge near the park (e.g., Mountain Gorilla View Lodge).

Activity: Optional gentle hike or cultural experience for kids.

Meals: Vegetarian and lactose-free meals at the lodge.

Day 8: February 27, 2025 - Gorilla Trekking

Morning: Adults and older kids (15+) trek to see the Silverback Gorillas, a breathtaking and life-changing experience.

For younger kids: Guided activities like visiting the nearby Gorilla Guardians Village.

Afternoon: Relax at the lodge after the trek.

Evening: Storytelling and stargazing activities for the whole family.

Day 9: February 28, 2025 - Lake Kivu

Morning: Drive to Lake Kivu for a day of relaxation by the water.

Accommodation: Four-star lakeside resort (e.g., Kivu Serena Hotel).

Activity: Swimming, boat ride, or family kayaking.

Meals: Lodge provides for special dietary needs.

Day 10: March 1, 2025 - Departure

Morning: Drive back to Kigali for your flight home.

Afternoon: Depart Kigali for Los Angeles via your connecting hub.

Key Notes:

Dietary requirements (vegetarian and lactose-free) will be accommodated at all accommodations.

All accommodations are family-friendly and four-star rated.

Kid-specific activities are included at various points to ensure they stay engaged and entertained.

Gorilla trekking permits should be booked in advance as they are limited.

Let me know if you'd like additional customization or help with bookings!

From here, of course, you can further request modifications to the itinerary, so you get exactly what you want (or as close to it as possible). If you want to try it out, I encourage you to do something similar—and if you want, tag me on Instagram (@therajeevkapur) with your results!

CHAPTER 4

CHAIN YOUR PROMPTS!

When you ask ChatGPT a simple question—such as what's the capital of New Hampshire, or how many Marvel movies have been produced, or how do you say "I would like chicken noodle soup" in Swedish—you're using a technique called **zero-shot prompting**. One simple prompt, one answer. You can do that for hours and pick up a lot of fun facts, right?

But you should go for more. If there's anything I want you to learn from this book, it's this: Zero-shot prompting is only the tip of the iceberg of what you can do with generative AI—and it's something you can already do with a web search. So, it's a waste of ChatGPT's talents. By utilizing various types of prompt chains, which we mentioned briefly in the last chapter, you can take on more complex and multistep projects as well as tailor ChatGPT's outputs more closely to what you're looking for.

This is going to be a big chapter, because we're about to identify the different kinds of prompt chains you can use to target certain kinds of results—and we'll also tell you how and when to leverage them to the best results. My main objective is not for you to memorize all this material, but to make you aware of the various ways you can put ChatGPT to work for you.

The Types of Prompt Chains

First, a formal definition: Prompt chains are structured approaches to guide AI reasoning by sequencing or combining multiple prompts in a specific way. In plain language, the more prompts you use, the more targeted and accurate your results, which is especially valuable when applying ChatGPT to more complicated tasks like problem-solving, decision-making, storytelling, and/or creating large projects like presentations and research papers.

Therefore, **prompt chaining** is the technique by which you break down complex tasks into a sequence of smaller, interconnected prompts, where each prompt builds on the outputs of previous ones. Think of it like an assembly line where each station handles a specific part of the task. Or, like an algebra teacher guiding a student step-by-step through a complicated formula. Perhaps most appropriately, think about cooking a dish by following a recipe. Each step (hopefully) takes you closer to a delicious result.

In the previous chapter, you saw an excellent example of prompt chaining when I guided ChatGPT to write a job application cover letter by giving it step-by-step instructions to get what I wanted. This is the basic chain prompting technique.

Besides zero-shot prompting, the following are the most common types of prompt chains and are meant for more specific uses.

- **Chain of Thought (CoT) Prompting**

  Sometimes a simple answer is not enough. Sometimes you want to understand how ChatGPT logically came to that answer, because (a) you just want to know, and (b) it will give you insight into how to solve other similar problems. Here's a simple example of how ChatGPT can both solve a math problem and explain the logic behind it simultaneously:

> *What is 47 x 42? Think step by step.*

Let's calculate 47 x 42 step by step:

Break 42 into 40 + 2.
Multiply 47 x 40:
47 x 40 = 1880.
Multiply 47 x 2:
47 x 2 = 94.
Add the results from steps 2 and 3:
1880 + 94 = 1974.

Final Answer: 47 x 42 = 1974.

You can use this technique with scientific queries as well as logic puzzles and even questions on debugging programming code. With CoT prompts, you can actually learn what it takes to resolve these kinds of questions, and you can get some background when you want it. For example, if you ask ChatGPT what caused World War I and ask it to explain its answer step by step, you'll get this response:

> *What were the causes of World War I? Explain step by step.*

1. The first major cause was the system of alliances, which divided Europe into opposing camps.
2. Next, militarism and the arms race created a climate of tension and competition.
3. Then, imperialism led to conflicts over colonies and global influence.
4. Finally, the assassination of Archduke Franz Ferdinand acted as the immediate trigger for the war.
5. These factors combined to lead to the outbreak of World War I.

To be honest, this is a very brief step-by-step summary I specifically requested. When I asked the first time, ChatGPT spewed out a few pages on the subject and I didn't want to put you to sleep here with a history lesson!

One other way to use CoT prompting is to help you brainstorm an open-ended question, one where there may not be one single "right" answer. Here's how that can work:

How can we reduce plastic waste in oceans? Think step by step.

1. Identify the main sources of plastic waste, such as single-use plastics and industrial waste.
2. Promote alternatives like biodegradable materials and reusable products.
3. Implement stricter regulations on waste disposal and recycling.

4. Increase public awareness through education campaigns.
5. Invest in technologies to clean up existing plastic in oceans.
6. By addressing these steps, we can reduce plastic waste effectively.

Simply put, CoT prompting is a great way to probe problems and issues with cold, hard logic and facts.

- **Few-Shot Prompting**

   With few-shot prompting, you provide ChatGPT with some examples of a task or query along with your request in a prompt. This helps establish the format, style, or type of response you want from ChatGPT. Here's a simple example:

> *Correct the grammar in the following sentences:*
>
> *1. "He don't know the answer." -> "He doesn't know the answer."*
> *2. "She go to the store yesterday." -> "She went to the store yesterday."*
> *3. "They is playing outside." -> "They are playing outside."*
>
> *Now correct this sentence: "We was watching a movie last night."*

"We were watching a movie last night."

Again, a very elementary example, but you get the idea. Few-shot prompts provide context by sharing examples of exactly what you're asking for. This is something I'm sure you've done in conversation. Think about when you're trying to describe a new TV series to someone. To give the other person a better idea of what the series is like, you compare it to other TV shows that are similar and familiar to that person. "You know, it's like *The Office* and *Modern Family*, with that fake documentary approach . . . " Your friend instantly gets what you're talking about, thanks to their familiarity with those other popular shows.

Here's a more advanced example of few-shot prompting, where I'm asking ChatGPT to write in a similar style to other examples I provide:

> *Write a brief product description for a smartwatch in the style of the two examples below:*
>
> 1. *"Smartphone: A sleek and powerful device with a 6.5-inch display, dual cameras, and all-day battery life."*
> 2. *"Wireless Earbuds: Compact earbuds with noise cancellation, long battery life, and crystal-clear sound quality."*

"Smartwatch: A stylish and durable wearable with a vibrant touchscreen, fitness tracking features, and all-day battery life."

As you can see, it delivered perfectly because I gave it a road map to follow. It knew how to structure the product description based on the other ones I fed to the app, and it replicated that style.

- **ReAct (Reasoning + Acting) Prompting**

  ReAct prompting combines logical reasoning and actionable steps. What exactly does that mean? I'm glad you asked! It means you're allowing ChatGPT to think through a problem and figure out how to solve it using outside resources if it feels it's necessary, such as an external tool or data it may not have acquired in its training. Here's a basic example:

> *What is 123 × 456? Think step by step and use a calculator if needed.*

Step-by-step calculation for 123 × 456:

1. Break the problem into components if needed, but in this case, directly compute 123 × 456.

2. Use a calculator to perform the multiplication.

Result: 123 × 456 = 56,088.

Very basic, as a matter of fact. But, using ReAct prompting, ChatGPT can handle something a whole lot more complicated than that, such as in the following example:

> *A customer wants a refund but their product is outside the return policy. Think step by step about how to handle this.*

Here's a step-by-step approach to handle this situation thoughtfully and professionally:

Step 1: Acknowledge the Customer's Concern

- *Begin by showing empathy and understanding.*
- ***Example****: "I understand how frustrating this must be, and I appreciate you bringing it to our attention."*
- Step 2: Review the Details
- *Politely confirm the specifics of the situation, including purchase date and policy terms.*
- ***Example****: "Let me take a moment to review your purchase and the details of our return policy to ensure I have all the information."*

Step 3: Explain the Return Policy

- *Clearly explain why the product is outside the return window but do so with kindness.*
- ***Example****: "Our return policy allows for returns within 30 days of purchase, and it looks like this product was purchased 45 days ago, so it's unfortunately outside the policy."*

Step 4: Offer Alternatives

- Provide solutions that balance policy adherence and customer satisfaction.
  - Offer store credit or an exchange if possible.
  - Provide a discount on a future purchase as a goodwill gesture.

- **Example**: *"While I can't process a refund, I'd be happy to offer you store credit for the amount, or a discount on your next purchase."*

Step 5: Escalate if Necessary

- *If the customer is still unhappy, escalate the issue to a supervisor or manager for further review.*
- **Example**: *"I understand this may not be the outcome you were hoping for. Let me connect you with a manager to see if there's anything else we can do."*

Step 6: End on a Positive Note

- *Thank the customer for their understanding and patience.*
- **Example**: *"We truly appreciate your business and understanding. Please let us know if there's anything else we can do to assist."*

This step-by-step approach ensures professionalism, adheres to policies, and strives to leave the customer feeling valued, even if the refund cannot be issued.

Based just on that short and sweet prompt, ChatGPT delivered a detailed guide to calming down even the angriest customer in the world.

The speed with which ChatGPT delivers a document like this is breathtaking, because it has the ability to "think" instantly and deliver a reasoned and intelligent answer, whereas you or I might take an hour or so to come up with all that content.

ReAct can provide all the options it thinks are available to help answer your question.

- **Reflection Prompting**

  At times, we all need to take stock of ourselves and assess whether we're doing a job correctly after we get specific feedback. Well, ChatGPT can even do that if you ask it to—and it will revise its output based on your input. In the below example, I asked for a synopsis of the Dickens classic, *A Tale of Two Cities.*

> *Summarize "A Tale of Two Cities" in three paragraphs.*

"A Tale of Two Cities" by Charles Dickens is a historical novel set during the tumultuous period of the French Revolution, weaving together themes of sacrifice, redemption, and the clash between justice and vengeance. The story begins in 1775, with England and France depicted as societies rife with corruption and inequality. The novel opens with the famous line, "It was the best of times, it was the worst of times," encapsulating the stark contrasts of the era. The plot follows the intertwining lives of several characters, including Charles Darnay, a French aristocrat who renounces his title; Dr. Alexandre Manette, a former prisoner of the Bastille; and Sydney Carton, a disillusioned English lawyer. Lucie Manette, Dr. Manette's compassionate daughter, serves as the moral center, tying the characters together.

The narrative explores the rising tensions in France as revolutionary fervor builds. Charles Darnay, despite his efforts to distance himself from his family's oppressive legacy, is drawn back to France to help a loyal servant. He is captured and sentenced to death by guillotine, branded as an enemy of the people due to his aristocratic lineage. Meanwhile, Sydney Carton, who bears a striking resemblance to Darnay and secretly loves Lucie, undergoes a transformation. Carton's journey from cynicism to selflessness becomes central to the story's theme of redemption.

In the climactic scenes, Carton switches places with Darnay, sacrificing his life to save the man Lucie loves. His famous final words, "It is a far, far better thing that I do, than I have ever done," reflect his ultimate act of redemption. The novel ends with hope and renewal for the surviving characters, juxtaposed against the violent backdrop of the Revolution. Dickens' portrayal of love, sacrifice, and the human cost of justice provides a poignant commentary on the social upheavals of his time.

Let's say I decided those paragraphs are too long. Also, maybe the summary seemed a little too complicated? So, I asked ChatGPT to make some changes:

Can you shorten the paragraphs and make it more readable?

"A Tale of Two Cities" by Charles Dickens is set during the French Revolution and explores themes of sacrifice, redemption, and justice. The story follows Charles Darnay, a French aristocrat who renounces his title; Dr. Alexandre Manette, a former prisoner of the Bastille; and Sydney Carton, a disillusioned English lawyer. Lucie Manette, Dr. Manette's compassionate daughter, ties the characters together. The novel opens with the famous line, "It was the best of times, it was the worst of times," reflecting the stark contrasts of the era.

As revolutionary tensions rise in France, Darnay returns to help a loyal servant but is arrested and sentenced to death because of his aristocratic lineage. Meanwhile, Sydney Carton, who resembles Darnay and secretly loves Lucie, finds purpose in his life through an act of selflessness. Carton's transformation becomes a central focus of the story.

In the dramatic conclusion, Carton sacrifices himself by taking Darnay's place at the guillotine to save him and Lucie. His famous final words, "It is a far, far better thing that I do, than I have ever done," symbolize his redemption. The novel concludes with hope for the survivors, set against the backdrop of the Revolution's chaos and violence. Dickens highlights love, sacrifice, and the cost of justice in a turbulent world.

And . . . voila! Just like magic, ChatGPT instantly spits out a version that's more to my liking. The takeaway here is you don't have to settle for results that aren't satisfying. Unlike a human who might grumble about having to make changes, ChatGPT couldn't care less—it'll just try to give you what you want without any hassle. (The day we really have to start worrying about AI is the day it starts complaining to us.)

- **Cascade Prompting**

  Cascade prompting involves breaking a complex task into much smaller steps, and, as with many of the other prompt chain types we've discussed, the output of one step serves as the input for the next.

  Here's an example of how cascade prompting works. I wanted ChatGPT to write a short story about friendship, and decided the first step I wanted to try was defining the characters. Here's how that went:

> *Describe two main characters for a short story about friendship.*

Character 1: Lily

Lily is a 13-year-old extrovert with a love for painting and bright colors. She is bubbly, adventurous, and has an uncanny ability to see beauty in even the smallest things, like the pattern on a butterfly's wings or the shape of clouds in the sky. Her energy often masks her insecurities about fitting in, as she feels misunderstood by many of her peers. She dreams of one day becoming an artist and bringing joy to others through her creations.

Character 2: Mia

Mia is a 12-year-old introvert who loves books, especially ones about science and space exploration. She is thoughtful, logical, and observant, preferring to spend her time stargazing or conducting small experiments in her backyard. Unlike Lily, Mia struggles to express her feelings openly and often worries about being seen as "too serious." She dreams of becoming an astronaut, exploring worlds beyond Earth.

Despite their differences, Lily and Mia form a deep bond when they discover a shared fascination with constellations and decide to create a massive mural of the night sky in their town, combining Lily's artistic talent with Mia's scientific precision. Their friendship helps them embrace their unique qualities and inspires others around them.

Now, that's pretty impressive considering the few details I gave ChatGPT. And, again, it instantly wrote out all that detail without hesitation.

For step 2, I decided to ask the question, where should this story take place?

Describe a setting where the story could take place.

Setting: The Overgrown Observatory

The story takes place in a small, forgotten observatory on the outskirts of town, hidden within a dense forest. Decades ago, the observatory was a hub for stargazers and scientists, but now it lies abandoned, its domed roof covered in vines and moss. Inside, the telescope still stands, dusty and rusted, but pointing eternally toward the heavens. Cracked walls are adorned with faded star charts, and the scent of old paper lingers in the air.

The observatory feels magical and mysterious, as sunlight streams through broken windows during the day, casting kaleidoscopic patterns on the floor. At night, the forest around it comes alive with the sounds of crickets and rustling leaves, while the open dome offers an unobstructed view of the glittering night sky. For Lily and Mia, this place becomes both a refuge and a canvas for their creative and scientific endeavors, embodying their growing friendship and shared dreams of exploring the universe—whether through art or science.

Again, a minimal prompt elicits enormous detail. So, let's keep going with our cascade prompting. Every great story requires conflict, so, your move, ChatGPT.

What conflict will the characters face in the story?

Conflict: Balancing Dreams and Fears

Lily and Mia discover an old, locked trunk hidden in the observatory's basement. Rumored to belong to the astronomer who built the observatory, the trunk is said to contain secrets about the stars or even maps to hidden celestial phenomena. Eager to uncover its contents, the two friends embark on a mission to solve the riddle etched into its lid.

However, their differences create tension. Lily's impulsive nature leads her to make risky decisions, like attempting to climb a rickety staircase for clues, while Mia's cautious approach causes delays and frustration. As they explore, they also face personal challenges—Lily must confront her fear of being seen as impractical, while Mia struggles with the idea of taking risks and letting go of perfection. Their conflicting approaches put their friendship to the test, forcing them to learn the value of compromise and trust.

The conflict deepens when they discover that solving the riddle requires combining their talents: Lily's creative thinking and Mia's analytical skills. Only by working together can they open the trunk and uncover the secrets it holds, transforming their struggles into a story of teamwork and mutual growth.

Sounds good. But how's this story going to come out? Only ChatGPT knows:

Write the climactic moment of the story.

Climactic Moment

Lily and Mia stand in the observatory's dusty basement, staring at the old trunk as the final piece of the riddle clicks into place. They've spent hours piecing together fragments of star charts and deciphering cryptic notes left by the astronomer. With trembling hands, Mia carefully aligns the last star symbol on the trunk's intricate lock mechanism.

As the lock clicks open, a faint hum fills the room, and a gust of cool air sweeps through the basement, carrying the scent of pine. Lily eagerly lifts the lid, revealing a collection of glowing vials, ancient maps, and a journal brimming with notes about constellations and theories of unseen stars. The light from the vials casts dancing patterns on the walls, illuminating their awestruck faces.

Their celebration is short-lived. A loud creak echoes from the floor above, and the rickety beams of the old observatory begin to groan under the weight of their movement. Dust and small debris rain down as the wooden staircase they used to descend shifts ominously.

"Lily, we need to get out of here!" Mia shouts, clutching the journal.

But before they can escape, a large beam collapses, blocking their path. Lily's quick thinking kicks in—she grabs an old telescope mount and uses it to pry open a side hatch they hadn't noticed before. With moments to spare, the two scramble out into the forest, clutching the journal and glowing vials, their hearts pounding.

As they catch their breath under the starlit sky, the realization hits them: they didn't just unlock the trunk—they unlocked the strength of their friendship, a bond forged through courage, trust, and the perfect balance of risk and caution.

From there, you can keep going with the short story process. It really is that easy. Which is why the Hollywood writers went a little crazy about the AI threat to their profession in 2023 and went on strike. Again, just know that with reflection prompting, you can have ChatGPT make changes to the story depending on how you want it to read. There will be no "creative differences," as they often say in the entertainment business.

Other Prompting Techniques

I've just shared with you the most complex prompt chain categories. Let's quickly review a few others that are fairly straightforward and don't require a lot of explanation or examples.

- **Goal-Driven Prompting**

  This is another way of tackling a sequential project, this time by specifying objectives and parameters at the get-go. Here are some examples of goal-driven prompts:

- ◆ "My goal is to teach 8th-grade students about the water cycle in a way that's interactive and engaging. Create a lesson plan that includes an introduction, a hands-on activity, and a closing discussion."
- ◆ "My goal is to explore Paris in three days while visiting major landmarks like the Eiffel Tower, the Louvre, and Notre Dame. Create a detailed itinerary that balances sightseeing and leisure time."
- ◆ "My goal is to save $500 this month while covering necessary expenses like rent, groceries, and utilities. Help me create a budget that identifies areas where I can cut costs and allocate savings."

- • **Role-Based Prompting**

  With role-based prompting, you ask ChatGPT to assume a different persona, so you can get an output with that perspective. Again, this is simple to do. Here's a sample role-based prompt:

  > *"Imagine you are a financial advisor. What advice would you give about saving for retirement?"*

  You can get more complex than that, as in the prompt below:

  > *"You are a professional copywriter specializing in marketing content. Write a product description for our new wireless headphones focusing on noise cancellation and battery life. Target audience: Tech-savvy professionals Tone: Premium but approachable. Word limit: 150 words."*

  Or. . . you can get silly.

> *Pretend you're Ariana Grande explaining Wicked in one paragraph.*

OMG, Wicked is just magical! It's the untold story of the witches of Oz, like way before Dorothy shows up. It's all about Elphaba, the "wicked" green witch, and Glinda, the "good" witch, and how their friendship and choices shaped their lives and the land of Oz. The music is iconic—"Defying Gravity" gives me chills every time—and the story is super emotional, with themes of acceptance, love, and standing up for what's right. Being part of this incredible world as Glinda is honestly such a dream come true!

You're welcome.

- **Exploratory Prompting**

  Exploratory prompting is used to encourage ChatGPT to discover various perspectives and possibilities, and to generate a wide range of ideas that can be used for brainstorming or creative thinking projects. It's mainly used to push the AI tech to not fall back on its usual patterns and to think outside its preprogrammed box. This is pretty easy to do if you use open-ended questions that may not have any specific right answer, forcing ChatGPT to come up with a variety of options for you to choose from and dig deeper if you want.

  For example, let's say you're contemplating writing a science fiction novel in which members of an alien race have three arms instead of our standard two. What would the impact of this be? ChatGPT can give you some ideas:

> *Briefly, what would the world be like if every person had three arms instead of two?*

If everyone had three arms, daily life would be more efficient, with multitasking becoming second nature—cooking, carrying, and texting all at once. Tools, vehicles, and clothing would be redesigned to accommodate the extra limb. Sports and music would evolve with new rules and instruments, while workplaces would become more productive. Social gestures and body language would expand, and art and culture would flourish with added creativity. Overall, the world would adapt to leverage the extra arm, transforming industries, infrastructure, and how we interact with one another.

You can also apply exploratory prompts to business brainstorming. Here's one suggested by ChatGPT:

> *If our business wanted to expand into a completely new market or industry, what innovative products or services could we offer that align with our strengths but address different customer needs? Think beyond our current offerings and consider future trends.*

- **Tree-of-Thought (ToT) Prompting**

    With ToT Prompting, you can explore multiple solutions simultaneously and have ChatGPT evaluate their pros and cons. Here's an example to show you how in-depth it can get:

I'm planning a vacation and want to choose between the mountains, the beach, and a city trip. Think step by step for each option, considering activities, cost, and overall experience. Then recommend the best option.

Option 1: The Mountains
- **Activities**: Hiking, camping, and stargazing. Great for nature lovers and relaxation.
- **Cost**: Generally affordable, especially if staying in cabins or camping.
- **Experience**: Peaceful, great for disconnecting from technology, but limited nightlife or cultural experiences.

Option 2: The Beach
- **Activities**: Swimming, sunbathing, water sports, and seaside dining. Perfect for unwinding and enjoying warm weather.
- **Cost**: Moderate, with potential high costs for beachfront accommodations.
- **Experience**: Relaxing and social but can be crowded during peak seasons.

Option 3: A City Trip
- **Activities**: Museums, restaurants, nightlife, and shopping. Ideal for culture and exploration.
- **Cost**: Can vary widely; accommodations and dining in major cities can be expensive.
- **Experience**: Energetic and diverse, but potentially overwhelming if seeking peace.

Evaluation and Recommendation:

- If you want relaxation and quiet, the mountains are the best choice.
- If you prefer warmth and social activities, the beach is ideal.
- If cultural experiences and a fast-paced environment excite you, a city trip is perfect.

Final Recommendation: Based on your interests (let me know if I'm wrong!), I'd suggest the beach for its balance of relaxation and activities, unless you're seeking peace, in which case the mountains would be better.

Each of the vacation suggestions is regarded as a "branch" in this particular tree-of-thought reply. As you can see, ChatGPT generates options, compares them and then makes a final recommendation. You don't have to follow that recommendation, because, as noted earlier, ChatGPT doesn't care whether you do or don't!

- **Verification Prompting**

Despite the mighty display of technology you've seen in this chapter, you must keep in mind that ChatGPT (as well as other AI apps) occasionally get it wrong—so you may want to ask it to check its work and report back to you.

These kinds of prompts fall under the umbrella of verification prompting:

"Check your previous calculation and confirm if it's correct."

"Review your explanation. Are the assumptions supported by evidence? If not, revise the response with stronger justification."

"Examine your argument for logical consistency and clarity. Are there any weak points or unsupported claims? If so, strengthen or revise them."

So, if you have a question about ChatGPT's responses, feel free to ask. It can be important to make sure you're getting the best and most accurate outputs from the AI.

Mixing It Up and Talking It Out

Did you know there's more than one way to communicate prompt chains to ChatGPT? And for ChatGPT to communicate back with you?

ChatGPT is now multimodal, which means it can process and generate multiple types of inputs and outputs, including text, images, and data, across a range of tasks and communication styles. Just download the app from OpenAI (there are a lot of similar apps out there, but the OpenAI one is the one you want).

For example, you can share an image and ask a question based on the image, like this:

Can you tell me why this car is leaking oil?

You can then use the persona technique to have ChatGPT explain how you might approach fixing the leak.

> *Act like an experienced mechanic. Tell me what steps you would take to identify the problem.*

As an experienced mechanic, here's how I'd approach diagnosing the oil leak:

1. Inspect the Leak Location
- Look under the car to identify where the oil is pooling or dripping from.
- Check if it's coming from the front, middle, or rear of the engine or oil pan.

2. Clean the Area

- Wipe off oil residue from the engine, oil pan, and surrounding components. This helps pinpoint the leak once fresh oil starts to seep out.

3. Check the Oil Level

- Verify the oil level to ensure it's not critically low. This also gives an idea of how much oil might be leaking.

4. Visual Inspection

- Inspect the following areas closely:
  - Oil pan gasket and drain plug – Look for loose bolts, stripped threads, or cracks.
  - Valve cover gasket – Common source in older cars due to gasket wear.
  - Oil filter – Check if it's tight and properly sealed.
  - Front and rear main seals – Look for oil tracking down the engine.
  - Hoses and connections – Inspect for cracks or loose fittings.

4. Run the Engine

- Start the engine and let it idle while observing for active leaks.
- Watch for oil dripping, especially around seals and gaskets, as the engine warms up.

5. Use a UV Dye and Light (If Needed)

- Add UV dye to the oil, run the engine, and use a UV light to trace the exact source of the leak.

6. Check for Pressure Issues

- Inspect the PCV valve for clogging. Excess crankcase pressure can force oil out of seals and gaskets.

7. Document Findings

- Note the exact location of the leak and assess the severity. For minor leaks, tightening bolts or replacing a gasket might suffice. For major leaks (e.g., from the rear main seal), plan for a more extensive repair.

Let me know if you'd like step-by-step guidance for any of these tasks!

So, yes, you can "feed" ChatGPT images, documents, and data for your prompt chain sessions. Not only that, but, with the ChatGPT phone app, you can now talk to it through your phone's app and actually have a conversation to try and solve a problem or get something you need done. It's pretty painless—as well as amazing.

With the interconnectedness of the multimodal feature, you can mix it up as much as you want. For example, in the last chapter, I had ChatGPT come up with a travel itinerary for a trip to Africa. Now, thanks to the multimodal feature, ChatGPT can pair that itinerary with a generated map or illustrations of the places you want to go. It can also create a chart with a narrative summary or mix text and visuals to present concepts in a compelling way.

In short, multimodal capability allows ChatGPT to work more like a human collaborator, blending the right tools to meet your specific needs.

Being Practical About Prompt Chains

Now, it's easy to become overwhelmed by all the different kinds of chain prompts I've explained in this chapter. But here's the thing: You don't have to carry around a list of them all to use ChatGPT effectively. As I noted earlier, my objective with this chapter was to show you just how many different tasks you can do with this level of generative AI technology, and how specifically you can instruct ChatGPT to accomplish them. When you use chain prompts properly, you enjoy these benefits:

- Better control over the output quality since you can review and adjust at each step
- More reliable handling of complex tasks that a single prompt can't convey
- Ability to inject your feedback or request modifications between steps
- Clearer organization of the thought process

The other point to remember is that you will undoubtedly combine some of these prompting techniques as you're working through a project or request. And that's a good thing, because you can guide ChatGPT to produce exactly what you want. But again, you must *tell* it what you want. For example, you might want the generative AI tool to write a full research paper about earthquakes. But if your prompt is simply, "Write a full research paper about earthquakes," it will probably not meet your requirements. Using prompt chaining will enable you to finesse ChatGPT to produce what you want. For example, you might want to start a prompt chain with this:

Generate an outline for a research paper on earthquakes.

Depending on how close the outline is to what you want, you might want to tweak it with a few more prompts. Then, when you feel it's ready, you can use another chain prompt to start the process of actually writing the paper:

> *Write the introduction section based on this outline.*

After the output appears, you may not like how ChatGPT writes the paper. The tone might be off. The language may not be quite right. You may want more sourcing. You can achieve all that and more with more prompts. Not only that, but you will be training ChatGPT in how you want the paper to be written, which it will remember as it writes more sections of it. That's why you want to construct a chain of prompts rather than start a new chat every time; the AI tool will be continuing on with the same task while keeping track of the parameters you've created for it to follow. Prompt chains are the AI version of a conversation—and they help get the job done. The more decisions you leave up to ChatGPT, the less likely it will generate exactly what you're looking for. The more detailed instructions you provide, the happier you'll be with the result.

And by the way, it might even be a path to a new career: AI start-ups are hiring prompt engineers at a starting salary up to $250,000. Netflix made waves last year when it was published that they were willing to pay $900K plus for experienced prompt engineers!

CHAPTER 5

PERSONAL PROMPTS

While most articles about generative AI focus on using it for professional purposes (which we'll tackle later in this book), there is a huge array of ways you can apply it to your personal life, including for self-reflection, personal growth, health and wellness, and even your personal relationships.

Does this seem weird? Even invasive? Well, since you're the only one who's going to see your ChatGPT outputs (unless you share an account with someone), you can feel free to spill your guts; in a sense, it's like getting advice from a trustworthy and experienced personal coach. In this chapter, we'll talk about a few of the many positive and proactive things you can do for yourself with this technology, beyond the examples I've already shared in this book.

One quick aside before I get into a few of the ways you can put ChatGPT to work for your life: Remember the OpenAI GPT store I mentioned earlier? Well, it features specialized GPTs that have been created for targeted tasks, like the ones I'll be discussing throughout the rest of this book. These GPTs can jumpstart your efforts, especially if you're a novice user. Many of them are free to use and they're all accessible at https://chatgpt.com/gpts. I'll identify some of them along the way.

And now, let's explore better living through ChatGPT.

Time Management and Personal Productivity

Increasingly, many of us feel like we don't have enough hours in the day to get everything done. But the culprit may be our inability to manage time effectively. A study by Acuity Training found that 82% of people lack a dedicated time management system,[8] which can lead to a sense of feeling completely overwhelmed, simply because you can't get a grip of what you should be doing when.

Here's where ChatGPT can come to the rescue. You can ask the app to design daily or weekly schedules while keeping your priorities in mind. Here's an example.

> *Help me create a schedule for tomorrow that prioritizes completing a presentation, attending a meeting, and going to the gym.*

Here's a sample schedule for tomorrow that balances your priorities effectively:

Morning
- 7:00 AM - 7:30 AM: Morning Routine (Breakfast, Prepare for the Day)
- 7:30 AM - 8:00 AM: Review Presentation Outline (Quick preparation to set the tone for the day)

---

8   https://learnopoly.com/105-time-management-statistics

- 8:00 AM - 9:00 AM: Gym (Energize your body and mind)

Midday
- 9:00 AM - 10:30 AM: Focused Work on Presentation (Tackle the most challenging parts while your energy is high)
- 10:30 AM - 10:45 AM: Short Break (Grab a coffee, stretch)
- 10:45 AM - 12:00 PM: Continue Presentation Work (Finalize and polish slides)
- 12:00 PM - 12:30 PM: Lunch Break
- 12:30 PM - 1:00 PM: Review Presentation (Final touch-ups and preparation)

Afternoon
- 1:00 PM - 2:00 PM: Attend the Meeting (Be punctual and engaged)
- 2:00 PM - 2:15 PM: Post-Meeting Notes (Capture key takeaways and action items)
- 2:15 PM - 3:00 PM: Practice Presentation (Run through to build confidence)

Evening
- 3:00 PM - 4:30 PM: Deep Focus Time for Other Tasks or Catch-Up Work (Optional time buffer)
- 4:30 PM - 5:00 PM: Reflection and Wrap-Up (Prepare for the next day)

As you can see, ChatGPT did a lot of heavy lifting from a very simple prompt. Should you want to try this, you can start with an equally brief prompt, then use prompt chains to fine-tune your schedule from there. You can also use frameworks like the Eisenhower Matrix or ABC prioritization to provide further organization. If you don't know what those two things are, ask ChatGPT and it'll be happy to tell you all you want to know (like, for instance, that the Eisenhower Matrix did indeed come from President Eisenhower).

Again, a more specialized GPT (available in the GPT store for paid users) can be very helpful here. Below is a screen shot of one of the top GPTs for this task and some prompts it suggests you can use to maximize your time:

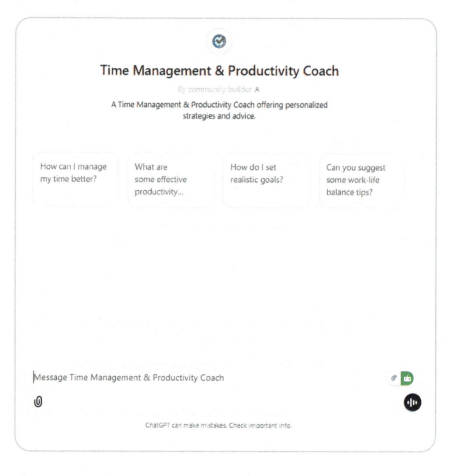

Personal Reflection

Now, if you're as busy as I just made you out to be, you might end up so scattered that you need a little help reconnecting with yourself. Here again, ChatGPT can help, with powerful methods of clarifying your thoughts, exploring ideas, and deepening your self-awareness. But for this process to work, you, of course, must be honest and share all your feelings. As an example, I told ChatGPT I was feeling stressed and anxious and asked what might be causing that. Its answer is below:

Stress and anxiety can stem from external pressures (work, relationships, finances), internal factors (perfectionism, self-doubt), physical issues (lack of sleep, poor diet), or unhelpful coping mechanisms.

Ask yourself:

- **When did it start?** Was there a specific trigger?
- **What makes it worse or better?** Are there patterns or routines affecting your mood?

I can help with mindfulness, stress management, or making a plan to address stressors. Let me know what feels most helpful!

You can also use ChatGPT if you want to try journaling. It can offer guidance, prompts, or even act as your personal virtual sounding board—and one that's nonjudgmental. Let's face it, our emotions can be messy, but ChatGPT can help you tap into your true feelings by:

- Suggesting thought-provoking questions to spark self-reflection.

- Offering prompts tailored to your goals, such as stress relief, gratitude, or self-discovery.
- Summarizing or clarifying your thoughts to bring focus and insight.

Here's what it had to say when I asked for some prompts along these lines:

Here are some self-reflection journaling prompts to help you explore your thoughts, emotions, and goals:

Understanding Yourself
1. What are three things I value most in life, and why?
2. When do I feel most like myself?
3. What personal strengths am I proud of, and how do I use them?
4. What fears hold me back, and how can I face them?
5. What does success mean to me?

Emotional Exploration
6. What emotions have been most present for me lately, and why?
7. How do I handle stress or anxiety, and what could I do differently?
8. When was the last time I felt truly happy, and what contributed to it?
9. What's one situation I'm struggling to let go of, and why?
10. How do I typically respond to criticism, and how does it affect me?

Growth and Goals

11. What lessons have I learned from recent challenges?
12. Where do I want to be in five years, and how can I start moving toward that?
13. What's a habit I'd like to change, and what small step could I take today?
14. What does my ideal day look like, and how does it align with my current life?
15. Who inspires me, and what qualities of theirs do I admire?

ChatGPT can also encourage you to journal consistently, if you set up reminders or motivational messages that will help you maintain your journaling habit. You can also create themed journaling routines, such as daily reflections or weekly check-ins. There are a lot of GPTs available that are strictly meant for journaling. Try a few of them out.

Setting Personal Goals

If you want to improve some aspect of yourself, ChatGPT can help you define clear, specific, and actionable goals. Whether it's losing weight, improving specific skills, learning a new language, or becoming a superhero (okay, maybe not that last one) ChatGPT can chart your path to progress.

For example, suppose you want to improve your fitness over the next three months. Maybe you want to get in shape for an athletic event or a high school reunion. Whatever the case, prompt chains will help get you what you want. Here's how I started the process:

> *Help me create a goal for improving fitness in 3 months.*

Here's a clear and actionable goal for improving fitness in 3 months:

Goal:
"Increase overall fitness by committing to a structured exercise routine 4–5 times a week, focusing on building strength, endurance, and flexibility, while maintaining a balanced diet and tracking progress."

Steps to Achieve This Goal:
1. Strength: Perform strength training 2–3 times a week (e.g., bodyweight exercises, weightlifting).
2. Endurance: Include cardio exercises like running, cycling, or swimming 2–3 times a week.
3. Flexibility: Add yoga or stretching routines 2 times a week.
4. Nutrition: Eat a balanced diet with sufficient protein, fruits, and vegetables.
5. Track Progress: Log workouts, monitor weight or body measurements, and celebrate milestones.

This goal is measurable, achievable, and adaptable to your starting fitness level. Let me know if you'd like to refine it further!

Now, maybe I want to break this down to find out what I should be doing on the daily to reach this goal. That's easy, as you're about to see.

> *What small daily actions can I take to improve my fitness?*

Here are small, manageable daily actions to improve your fitness:

1. **Move More:** Take a 15–30 minute walk or stretch during breaks.
2. **Hydrate:** Drink at least 8 glasses of water daily to stay energized.
3. **Snack Smart:** Swap processed snacks for fruits, nuts, or veggies.
4. **Strength Exercises:** Do a quick 10-minute routine (e.g., push-ups, squats, planks).
5. **Cardio Burst:** Add a short burst of activity like jumping jacks or a brisk jog.
6. **Stretching:** Spend 5–10 minutes stretching, especially after sitting for long periods.
7. **Sleep Well:** Aim for 7–9 hours of sleep to support recovery.
8. **Plan Meals:** Prep balanced meals with protein, whole grains, and vegetables.
9. **Track Activity:** Use a fitness tracker or app to log steps, workouts, or water intake.
10. **Mindfulness:** Practice deep breathing or meditation to reduce stress, which can impact fitness.

Consistently incorporating these actions can lead to noticeable improvements over time.

And how do I hold myself accountable? As always, ChatGPT has the answers:

> *Suggest ways to monitor my progress and stay consistent.*

Here are effective ways to monitor your progress and stay consistent with your fitness goals:

Monitoring Progress

1. **Track Workouts:** Use a fitness app or journal to log exercises, sets, reps, and durations.
2. **Measure Physical Changes:** Record body measurements, weight, or progress photos weekly or biweekly.
3. **Set Milestones:** Break your goal into smaller milestones, like increasing weights or running distance.
4. **Monitor Health Metrics:** Use a fitness tracker to track steps, heart rate, and sleep patterns.
5. **Keep a Nutrition Log:** Record meals to ensure balanced and consistent eating habits.

Staying Consistent

1. **Create a Schedule:** Set specific times for workouts and treat them as non-negotiable appointments.
2. **Find Accountability:** Share your goals with a friend or join a fitness group to stay motivated.
3. **Celebrate Wins:** Reward yourself for hitting milestones with non-food-related treats, like new workout gear.

4. **Make It Fun:** Incorporate activities you enjoy, like dancing, hiking, or playing sports.
5. **Be Flexible:** If life gets busy, adjust your plan but don't abandon it—shorter sessions still count.
6. **Reflect Regularly:** Revisit your progress weekly to assess what's working and where to adjust.

One last word: Be careful not to give ChatGPT too much control of your life—remember it can get some things wrong. In general, however, its advice is pretty reliable.

Reviewing Relationships

Yes, ChatGPT can even help with your personal relationships by providing thoughtful guidance and suggestions to improve them. If you want a GPT that's specifically designed for your gender, that's also an option; and, there are GPTs for LGBTQ folks as well. Below, you'll see one GPT (available in the GPT store) focused firmly on relationships, with suggestions for prompts to get started or continue chatting, if you've already begun a "conversation" with the Personal Relationships Navigator.

Personal Relationships Navigator

By Christian Reichert

Aides in Personal Relationship Management by organizing key personal data.

Lifestyle	**10+**
Category	Conversations

Conversation Starters

Tell me about a new person you met.	Update me on your recent conversation with John.
What should I remember about Sarah?	Remind me of the promise I made to Alex.

Capabilities

✓ Web Search

✓ DALL·E Images

ChatGPT can offer relationship help in the following areas:

- **Improving Communication**

  ChatGPT can help craft clear, empathetic messages for difficult conversations, as well as offer advice on how to express feelings effectively. It can also suggest ways to actively listen and understand others better.

ChatGPT can also help you communicate effectively with people who may not speak your language. It can translate most languages—including sign language, if you provide it with video. It can also instruct you how to sign what you want to tell the other person.

- **Resolving Conflicts**

  Are you having a disagreement with someone close to you? Generative AI can provide strategies to de-escalate arguments and ratchet down hard feelings as well as offer neutral perspectives so you can consider both sides of an issue.

- **Building Connections**

  GPTs can suggest activities or ideas to strengthen bonds with friends, family, or partners. They can also provide conversation starters and ways to deepen meaningful discussions.

- **Assessing Your Emotions**

  Relationships can really rock your mental boat and sometimes you're not sure *how* to feel. When that happens, GPTS can help you identify and process your feelings in challenging situations, as well as offer suggestions for managing stress, anxiety, or emotional triggers in relationships.

- **Making Meaningful Moves**

  Sometimes, it's hard to think of ways to dazzle someone on a date or on a special occasion. So, let ChatGPT think for you. It can help you brainstorm ideas for thoughtful gifts, date ideas, or ways to make a celebration really stand out.

But remember, it's all about the prompt. So, give it details on what help you need, get the response, and continue with chain prompting. This is also one area where using personas, which we talked about earlier in this book, really makes a huge difference. The more ChatGPT "understands" who you are, the better advice it can provide.

As you can see, there's a lot you can do with ChatGPT to up your personal game. But again, don't leave everything human up to something that's not human. ChatGPT can be an excellent supportive resource, but it's important to combine its advice with your intuition and real-life experiences.

Then again, there are signs that AI just might have some traces of humanity baked into its cake. A team of AI researchers at Google and Stanford University used ChatGPT to create 25 "generative agents," or unique personalities with identities and goals, and placed them into a virtual town they named Smallville, named after the town that Clark Kent grew up in before he became Superman. To create the Smallville residents, the team assigned each one of them a one-paragraph prompt for ChatGPT that included the character's memories, goals, relationships, and jobs. The "people" then began interacting independently in the virtual town setting. They actually began gossiping about each other and creating drama in the process. They also began building relationships where they would remind each other of things that had happened to them earlier in the simulation, as well as creating events that they would all attend.[9] None of this social

---

9 https://www.thedailybeast.com/google-and-stanford-researchers-used-chatgpt-to-invent-a-small-virtual-town?via=ios

activity was a part of their "programming." So that may be a sign that AI understands us more than we think it does.

In the next chapter, we're going to keep it all in the family—and show you how to use ChatGPT to manage yours!

CHAPTER 6

THE FAMILY THAT CHATGPTS TOGETHER . . .

Who doesn't want some help with running their household?

That's especially true if you work, your significant other works, you have kids in school, and maybe even a pet or two. You likely don't need AI to determine that the two things you're constantly short on are time and energy.

While there's not much specific data on the number of families using ChatGPT for household tasks at the moment, the tool is gaining in popularity among parents seeking to streamline daily responsibilities. Not everyone is anxious to convert, but Kate Anderson, an online blogger, is one mother who has welcomed AI into her home life:

Motherhood is always busy. . . . All three of my kids play sports, summer planning is in full-swing and there are so many celebrations. It is overwhelming to juggle everything. My husband and I both work full-time and I am lucky enough to work from home . . . now that we have three kids in school with 1-2 activities a kid, our lives are in complete overdrive. After school is a carpool shuffle between my husband, me and sometimes some lovely friends shuttle our kids around the area from baseball to lacrosse to gymnastics or rock climbing. It's a lot.

The use cases of how ChatGPT can help at work are endless, but what I was most surprised to learn was how it helped me in my personal life. . . . I started asking questions that were keeping me up at night. The never-ending list of parenthood that runs through your head at all hours of the day, but most particularly at 3 am in the morning. My list, which was in no way exhaustive, included the following:

- *What should we do for a week in Spain for spring break?*
- *Recommend a weeknight dinner that a 9-year-old can make.*
- *What should I bring for brunch I'm invited to this weekend?*
- *How do I think of fun lacrosse drills to do for 3rd/4th grade girls for two 1-hour practices every week for 12 weeks?*
- *What is an age-appropriate chore chart for a 9-year-old including a breakdown of the steps for each chore?*
- *What is a location for my husband's family to go on vacation where we can all fly direct?*[10]

---

10   https://www.mother.ly/career-money/work-and-motherhood/benefits-of-chatgpt-for-parents/

Well, you can see why Anderson couldn't sleep. And you can also see how getting thoughts on all those random questions might actually help her get forty winks. Those are the kinds of rewards Anderson has been able to reap since she started leaning heavily on ChatGPT. It's helped her with those ongoing daily demands that no working parent ever quite conquers. With ChatGPT, you can at least make a good run at meeting them all, and in this chapter, we'll offer some concrete suggestions on how to do just that.

Household Organization

For moms, ChatGPT might be a godsend, because the responsibilities of mothering are punishing these days—58% of moms say they are primarily responsible for the duties of running a household and caring for children.[11] While ChatGPT clearly can't change a diaper or put a Band-Aid on a kid's boo-boo, it can help with the kinds of tasks that Anderson asked AI to explore for her when she first began trying out generative AI. Anderson estimated in her first week of using ChatGPT that the app saved her at least five to ten hours of work—as well as one to three hours of insomnia, due to stressing about that work.

Well, let's dig into that work and offer some specific examples of how ChatGPT helped Anderson and how it might be able to help you.

Nine Ways to Make Parenting Easier with ChatGPT

You might think AI can't make a dent in the demands of raising kids. Well, believe it or not, ChatGPT has a lot to offer in terms of eliminating some of the drudgery and mental strain you have to endure if you're a parent. (Pro tip: Some of these tasks are also ones that adults without

---

11   https://www.mother.ly/state-of-motherhood/

kids need to do, so I suggest you at least look over these nine ways, as they will continue to demonstrate all you can do with ChatGPT.)

1. Fill Out Forms

Anybody who's had to enroll a child in school or take them to a doctor knows that filling out forms is a time-consuming, boring, and repetitive task—especially when half the time the people you're filling out the forms for already have most of the information. Well, here's a case where ChatGPT provides a quick and easy fix. Simply copy and paste the form into ChatGPT and put in this prompt:

> *"Can you ask me these questions one by one and compile my answers into the form format?"*

This won't be life-changing, but it will save you some time and energy. ChatGPT can help you fill in details like emergency contacts or medical history without missing a beat, so you can reclaim at least a few minutes from your busy day. And ChatGPT will continue to store the information you've already fed it, so you don't have to reenter everything for each form. I'll show you in a little bit how that memory function works.

2. Do Creative Brainstorming

Your kids are tired of the same old tales in their storybooks. Maybe they can't relate to them. And maybe they're asking you to come up with your own stories. Well, sometimes after a long hard day, the creativity doesn't exactly flow. That's when you can use ChatGPT to be your own personal Brothers Grimm.

Let's say I have a young daughter named Daisy who loves unicorns, jellybeans, and rainbows. And I tell all that to ChatGPT in the following prompt:

> *"I have a young daughter named Daisy who loves unicorns, jellybeans, and rainbows. Can you write a very brief story about a brave unicorn named Daisy that involves those other things?"*

Here's the story it generated all on its own:

Memory updated

Daisy the Brave Unicorn and the Jelly Bean Rainbow

Once upon a time, in a magical meadow, there was a brave unicorn named Daisy with a shimmering silver horn and a heart full of kindness. One day, the sky grew dark, and the Rainbow Bridge—made of sparkling colors—suddenly disappeared! Without it, the land's magic would fade.

Daisy knew what to do. She galloped across fields of candy flowers and up the Gumdrop Hills until she found the Rainbow Cloud, where the colors were hidden inside... a giant jar of enchanted jelly beans! But the beans were scattered, and a grumpy cloud troll guarded the jar.

"Only the bravest unicorn can put the colors back," growled the troll.

Daisy smiled. "I can do it!"

She used her horn to sort the jelly beans: reds with reds, blues with blues, yellows with yellows. With every color she placed, the rainbow began to reappear, shining brighter and brighter.

Finally, the troll handed Daisy the last magical bean—a glittering rainbow jelly bean. She tossed it into the sky, and whoosh! the Rainbow Bridge burst back into life, filling the meadow with light.

The troll cheered, and Daisy trotted home, her silver horn glowing with pride. From that day on, everyone knew Daisy as the unicorn who brought back the magic—one jelly bean at a time.

And, of course, she celebrated with a big bag of jelly beans under the brightest rainbow she'd ever seen.

Pretty cool, right? But I want you to note one more detail from that last screenshot. Right by the ChatGPT icon in the top left, you'll see shaded type that reads "Memory updated." What that means is ChatGPT took note of the information you provided and added it to its memory, so the more you tell it about Daisy, the less you'll have to tell it next time. You can see what it retained in the next screenshot:

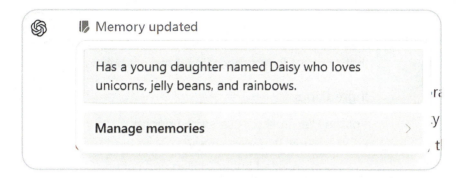

And you'll also note the "Manage memories" underneath the retained information in bold type. Click on that to delete memories you *don't* want ChatGPT to hang onto.

There are tons of other family brainstorming projects you can perform besides creating personalized bedtime stories. For example, ChatGPT can suggest ideas for alternative activities when rain disrupts outdoor plans.

3. Generate Fun and Educational Quizzes

You can turn learning into a game by asking ChatGPT to generate quizzes. For example, if your child is learning about planets, you can ask ChatGPT for trivia questions like, "What's the largest planet in our solar system?" Then, make it a friendly competition—winner gets to pick the next family movie or something similar.

4. Provide (and Adjust) Recipes

If you need a simple recipe for dinner, ChatGPT can provide it. Just specify all your wants in the prompt or in a prompt chain. You can even make it short and simple, like so:

Provide a tasty recipe for apple pie

Here's a classic, easy, and delicious **apple pie recipe** that's perfect for any occasion. Let's get baking!

Ingredients

For the Pie Crust (or use store-bought):
- 2 ½ cups all-purpose flour
- 1 cup unsalted butter, chilled and cubed
- 1 teaspoon salt
- 1 teaspoon sugar
- 6-8 tablespoons ice water

Obviously, there was more to the recipe than this. But maybe I just looked and saw I didn't have very much flour—as a matter of fact, I only have one cup instead of 2½. Can ChatGPT help me out? Of course it can!

I only have one cup of flour for the apple pie recipe. Is there a workaround?

Yes, there's definitely a workaround if you only have 1 cup of flour for the apple pie recipe! Here are a couple of options to make it work:

Make a Single-Crust Pie

Instead of a top and bottom crust, make an open-faced pie.
- Use your 1 cup of flour to make a single crust for the bottom of the pie.

- Follow the recipe for the apple filling, but instead of covering it with another crust, sprinkle the filling with a crumble topping:
  - Mix together 3 tablespoons of flour, 3 tablespoons of oats (or more flour), 2 tablespoons of sugar, and 2 tablespoons of cold butter to form crumbs. Sprinkle on top before baking.
  - This gives a delicious, crunchy finish without the need for extra flour.

I only included one of the options (there were two more provided) but this demonstrates how ChatGPT can help you problem-solve, even when it comes to cooking and baking. If your kids are old enough, they can even use ChatGPT to help them cook and maybe give you a break from the kitchen.

5. Make To-Do Lists and Instructions

Say you've got a new babysitter coming over and there are a few things you want her to keep track of, to keep your kids on your preferred schedule. All you have to do is dictate the tasks and instructions to the ChatGPT app, using your phone. For example, when preparing babysitter instructions, you could say, "Dinner is at 6, bath at 7, bedtime at 8. Snacks are in the pantry, but no sugar before bedtime." ChatGPT will turn what you say into clear, bullet-pointed instructions grouped by category. Now all you have to do is get that babysitter to read them . . .

6. Organize Shopping Lists

What you just did for the babysitter you can do for yourself. Practice walking around the kitchen with your ChatGPT app open, looking in the refrigerator and pantry, and telling it what items you're out of and need to replace at the store. ChatGPT will not only turn those items into a shopping list, but it can also organize them into categories such as "Produce," "Dairy," "Baking," etc., so you can navigate the store aisles like a pro!

7. Manage Family Events

If you're an overscheduled family, then you need someone to help you keep track of birthdays, sports practices and games, doctor appointments, and other time-sensitive obligations. So, let ChatGPT be your personal assistant. Tell it details like, "Jake's soccer game, Saturday at 2 p.m.," or "Dentist appointment for Belinda, Tuesday at 3 p.m.," and ChatGPT can send reminders or even help you draft a weekly schedule so nothing slips through the cracks. And again, you can adjust, add, or delete entries with prompt chains.

8. Plan Family Trips

Overwhelmed by vacation planning? Share your destination, travel dates, and preferences with ChatGPT, and it will create an itinerary, just like it did for me back in chapter 3. For a trip to the beach, it might suggest, "Day 1: Relax on the shore. Day 2: Visit the aquarium. Day 3: Explore local seafood restaurants." It can even make sure spots are kid-friendly and help you keep costs down with money-saving travel ideas.

9. Help with Homeschooling and Homework

Whether you're teaching your kids full time at home or just anxious to help them through some horrendous homework at night, ChatGPT has a lot to offer when it comes to educating your little students. For example, I asked it to explain adding fractions and it provided a perfect step-by-step answer along with an example:

Can you briefly explain how to add fractions with an example?

Sure! To add fractions, follow these steps:

1. Make the denominators (bottom numbers) the same if they're different.
2. Add the numerators (top numbers) while keeping the denominator the same.
3. Simplify the result if possible.

Example: 1/4 + 2/3

1. Find a common denominator. For 4 and 3, the least common denominator is 12.
   - Convert 1/4: Multiply top and bottom by 3 → 3/12.
   - Convert 2/3: Multiply top and bottom by 4 → 8/12.
2. Add the numerators: 3 + 8 = 11.
   - Keep the denominator (12) the same.
3. Final answer: 11/12.

So, 1/4 + 2/3 = 11/12.

You can also use ChatGPT to create flashcards and, as we already discussed, quizzes. ChatGPT can also be an engaging and interactive way to educate your kids. Just make sure they're actually learning with it and not just using the app to supply all the answers! (For an AI app specifically designed for students and educators, check out http://www.khanmigo.ai).

There are also a lot of creative and exciting things you can do with ChatGPT to make family time more efficient and fun. You can ask it for topics to discuss at the dinner table, a poem about your family using the specific information you've provided about everyone, or, to keep it simple, simply entertain the kids with a groan-worthy knock-knock joke.

> *Write a knock-knock joke.*

Sure! Here's one for Daisy:

Knock, knock!

Who's there?

Unicorn.

Unicorn who?

Unicorn believe how much Daisy loves rainbows and jelly beans!

Like I said—ChatGPT remembers!

Next chapter? We're going to go to work—and show you how to leverage ChatGPT on the job.

CHAPTER 7

PROFESSIONAL PROMPTS

Just how business friendly is generative AI?

The answer is, *very.* According to the global business consultancy McKinsey and Company, roughly 72% of organizations report that they're using AI in at least one business function—and 65% are regularly using generative AI, nearly double the percentage from their previous survey ten months earlier.[12] In other words, AI usage at companies is skyrocketing and there's a lot more growth to come. And these companies are already seeing material benefits from generative AI, enabling them to both cut costs and increase revenue with the new technology.

So, shouldn't you get in on the boom?

---

12 https://www.mckinsey.com/capabilities/quantumblack/our-insights/the-state-of-ai

In this chapter, we'll take a quick look at how ChatGPT is being put to work for business purposes and then discuss how to use prompts to leverage its power to the fullest, no matter what kind of work you do.

Doing Business with AI

With ChatGPT, you can do a lot more work with a lot less effort. Here are a few quick examples of how it's being used at the corporate level:

- **Market Research:** You can get instant data-driven insights that allow you to make more informed and strategic decisions. AI can also predict trends and consumer behavior. (Reminder, the paid version of ChatGPT also gives you access to the extremely advanced Deep Research feature as well.)

- **Efficiency:** Generative AI can automate repetitive and time-consuming tasks, like data entry, scheduling, resume screening, and even responding to basic customer inquiries.

- **Personalization:** AI enables businesses to offer personalized experiences to customers and employees by analyzing their preferences and behaviors and providing customized marketing and product recommendations, like you see if you're a customer of companies like Amazon and Netflix.

- **Customer Insights:** AI can evaluate customer feedback and social media posts, then synthesize the data, helping businesses understand their customers' needs and preferences, leading to better product development and customer service strategies.

- **Brainstorming:** Looking for a jolt of creative thinking? Want to shake up your perspective on your company, your work, or your career? ChatGPT can help you with that as well, offering suggestions and ideas that might never have otherwise occurred to you.

- **Strategic Planning:** Just like the brainstorming function, using ChatGPT for strategic planning can help you see profitable and sustainable business paths you may be unaware of. Feed the app as much info about your business as possible (remember, you can upload documents for it to review and remember), and use specific prompts to create a plan to move your organization forward.

Not every business has jumped on the AI train yet. While AI adoption is growing, the extent and sophistication of its usage can vary widely among businesses. Some companies may be in the early stages of exploring AI capabilities, while others have fully integrated AI into their operations.

This isn't to say AI is foolproof! McDonald's worked with IBM for three years to create AI technology that would enable it to handle the burger chain's drive-through orders, but that effort was cancelled in June 2024. Why? Because, all of a sudden, videos started popping up on social media created by frustrated customers who couldn't get the AI to understand their orders. One TikTok video in particular went viral: It featured two people repeatedly pleading with the AI tech to stop adding more Chicken McNuggets to their order. Instead, it tried to put through an order of 260 nuggets. That was enough for McDonald's.[13] (However, Wendy's is currently trying to do the same thing, as we detailed earlier in this book. Hopefully, no one will end up with a thousand Frosties!)

So, that's some of the "big picture" AI usage going on right now at the world's biggest companies. Obviously, generative AI is going to have an increasingly profound effect on the workplace—which is exactly why

---

13 https://www.cio.com/article/190888/5-famous-analytics-and-ai-disasters.html

you should get an idea of how you can use it for your own professional benefit. I'll be helping you with that effort by going from the global to the granular to show you how to work with prompts to accomplish specific professional tasks.

But first . . . let's talk about making generative AI a little more . . . human.

Humanizing AI Outputs

If you're familiar with the classic Brad Pitt movie, *Fight Club,* then you know the first rule of Fight Club is you do not talk about Fight Club. Well, let's modify that slightly for our purposes to this: The first rule of using generative AI tools like ChatGPT is you do not want anyone to know you're using generative AI. If you use ChatGPT to write business emails, posts, cover letters, and so forth, you want it to sound like you did it on your own, right?

So, before we get into the specifics of business tasks we can perform with the help of ChatGPT, let's first talk about how to make its outputs sound as human as possible. Even more to the point, let's make those outputs sound as much like *you* as possible. While ChatGPT outputs are continuing to improve and read more naturally, you may still want to refine their tone, context, and phrasing. Here are the three main ways to make that happen:

- **Share Your Style**

  Use a prompt to tell ChatGPT how you typically communicate and say you want it to mimic your tone, like this one:

  > *"Replicate my communication style, which is a direct and conversational tone without any overly dramatic statements or complex phrasing but adding some humor."*

- **Reveal Any Signature Phrases or Expressions**

  If you have some common expressions you use that people are aware of, let ChatGPT know, and it will use those expressions in its outputs. An example prompt:

  > *"I use the expressions 'Here's the deal,' and 'That's the bottom line' often. Please use each of these once in your output."*

- **Give ChatGPT Samples of Your Writing**

  What's really helpful is giving ChatGPT a taste of how you write and express yourself. So, feel free to upload documents you have personally written (just use the paper clip icon on ChatGPT to attach files—it's to the left of the prompt box), so it can analyze them and lock in to your style.

- **Specify the Tone**

  Finally, and most crucially, you're going to want to tailor the tone to the task. Sometimes you want to lay down the law—other times, you want to keep it casual and fun. Whatever style you want, ChatGPT is down to deliver. And I've got receipts. First, let's give ChatGPT a relatively straightforward task.

  > *Write a 250-word paragraph on how to improve sales at a company.*

 Improving sales at a company starts with understanding your customers and aligning your offerings to their needs. Begin by analyzing your current customer base and market trends to identify gaps and opportunities. Invest in training your sales team to refine their skills, focusing on product knowledge, communication, and relationship-building techniques. Establish clear, measurable sales goals and track performance with reliable metrics to ensure accountability and progress. Leveraging technology, such as customer relationship management (CRM) software, can streamline processes and provide valuable insights into customer behavior. Additionally, prioritize building strong customer relationships by emphasizing value over selling. Personalize interactions, listen to their pain points, and tailor your solutions to their needs. Marketing and sales should work hand in hand to generate qualified leads; utilizing data-driven campaigns that resonate with target audiences. Offering incentives, such as discounts or loyalty programs, can encourage repeat business and referrals. Don't overlook the importance of feedback; actively seek input from both customers and your sales team to identify areas for improvement. Regularly evaluate your sales process to eliminate inefficiencies and adapt to changing market conditions. Consider expanding your product line or services if there's demand, but ensure your team is equipped to sell effectively. Finally, fostering a strong company culture that motivates and rewards high-performing employees can significantly boost morale and productivity. By taking a comprehensive, customer-focused approach, companies can create a sustainable sales strategy that drives revenue growth and strengthens their market position.

That's perfectly fine. But let's try loosening things up a little.

Boosting sales at a company comes down to really understanding your customers and giving them what they need. Start by taking a close look at who's buying from you now and what's happening in the market—this will help you spot opportunities you might be missing. Make sure your sales team is sharp by providing training that focuses on the basics: knowing your product inside and out, connecting with customers, and building solid relationships. Set clear goals and keep track of how things are going with tools like CRM software that can also give you a better idea of what your customers want. When interacting with customers, focus on being helpful rather than just making the sale. Listen to their problems and show them how your product or service can solve them. Marketing and sales should work together to bring in leads that are ready to buy, using campaigns that speak directly to your target audience. Offering things like discounts or loyalty perks can keep people coming back and encourage them to spread the word. Don't forget to get feedback from both your team and your customers—it's the best way to know where you can do better. If it makes sense, consider adding new products or services, but make sure your team is ready to sell them. And finally, keep your team motivated with rewards and a positive culture. By focusing on your customers and staying adaptable, you'll see those sales numbers climb.

Better. But now, let's try to have some fun with it.

> *Now make the tone informal and humorous.*

Want to crank up sales? It's all about knowing your customers and making them feel like you've got exactly what they need—even if they didn't know they needed it. First, figure out who's buying your stuff and why, and then spot the gaps where you can sneak in and say, "Hey, we've got you covered!" Next, make sure your sales team isn't winging it—they need to know the product better than they know the plot of their favorite TV show. Also, set some goals they can actually hit, and track progress with tools like CRM software (because spreadsheets are so last century).

When talking to customers, don't go all "hard sell." No one likes that. Instead, listen to their gripes and show them how your product can make their lives better—bonus points if you can make them laugh along the way. Get your marketing team on board too; they're your sales wingmen. Run campaigns that make people go, "Wow, I need that in my life!" Sweeten the deal with discounts or loyalty perks, because who doesn't love a good freebie?

Ask for feedback like it's gossip about your favorite celebrity—eagerly and often. If you see a chance to add a new product or service, great! But don't throw your team into the deep end without a floatie. And remember, happy employees = productive employees, so reward the heck out of them when they crush it. Do all that, and you'll be raking in the sales in no time.

Okay, maybe we've gone too far. After all, we don't want people to laugh this off, right? So, let's try a third approach. . .

> *Now make the tone serious and somber.*

Improving sales at a company requires a clear, disciplined approach and a deep understanding of both the market and customer needs. It begins with a comprehensive analysis of the current customer base, identifying gaps in service or unmet demands. Sales teams must be rigorously trained, not just in product knowledge but in empathetic communication and the art of building lasting relationships. Goals should be carefully set, measured, and reviewed with precision, utilizing tools like CRM software to monitor progress and gain insights into customer behavior. Each customer interaction must prioritize understanding and addressing their challenges, demonstrating the true value of what you offer rather than simply pushing for a transaction.

Marketing efforts must align seamlessly with sales, creating campaigns grounded in data and designed to attract qualified leads. Loyalty programs or other incentives should be thoughtfully implemented to encourage repeat business and referrals, but only if they genuinely enhance the customer experience. Seeking feedback is crucial; it often reveals hard truths about shortcomings that need to be addressed. Expanding the product line or services may be necessary to remain competitive, but such decisions should be made with caution and thorough preparation.

Ultimately, the success of a sales strategy hinges on the dedication and morale of the team executing it. A strong, supportive company culture is not a luxury—it is a necessity. Sales improvements require more than effort; they demand commitment, reflection, and the ability to adapt to a constantly changing landscape. Without these, growth remains elusive.

- With any of the above examples—or anything else you ask ChatGPT to write—you can continue to refine and provide specific instructions as to what you want changed. It's really that easy. You can even make it more personal—sort of:

Can you add a personal insight to this that sounds like something I experienced?

Improving sales at a company requires a clear, disciplined approach and a deep understanding of both the market and customer needs. I remember a time early in my career when our sales team faced a crisis: revenue had flatlined, and morale was at an all-time low. It was clear we needed more than just pep talks—we needed a plan. We started by analyzing our customer base and discovered something surprising: we were targeting the wrong audience. Adjusting our focus was humbling, but it worked. We invested in training the team, not just on product knowledge, but on active listening and problem-solving. Goals became clearer, and with the help of CRM software, we could track and celebrate small wins.

Each customer meeting turned into an opportunity to understand their challenges and truly offer solutions. I'll never forget one client who said, "You're the first person to actually listen instead of just trying to sell me something." That stuck with me. Marketing and sales began working hand-in-hand, crafting campaigns that resonated with the new target audience. Loyalty programs brought customers back, and regular feedback—both from clients and the team—became a cornerstone of our strategy. Expanding our offerings came later, but only after ensuring we could deliver with excellence.

That experience taught me the power of aligning people, tools, and strategies with a shared vision. It's not just about numbers—it's about building trust, both

> internally and externally. When done right, the results are transformative.

And there you have it: A manufactured personal anecdote (I only gave it the information I put into the prompt, so it fabricated the whole thing). And again, all the above outputs were composed within seconds of my entering the prompt. And by the way, the more you interact with ChatGPT with chain prompts on a project like this, the more easily it can mimic how you express yourself. If you provide ChatGPT with consistent guidance, examples, and feedback, it can make its responses increasingly indistinguishable from your own writing.

In general, there are other ways you can instruct ChatGPT to write more naturally. AI expert Ben Attanasio suggested using the following prompts in a 2024 Reddit post:[14]

- **Use simple language:** Write plainly with short sentences.
  - *Example: "I need help with this issue."*

- **Avoid AI-giveaway phrases:** Don't use clichés like "dive into," "unleash your potential," etc.
  - *Avoid: "Let's dive into this game-changing solution."*
  - *Use instead: "Here's how it works."*

- **Be direct and concise:** Get to the point; remove unnecessary words.
  - *Example: "We should meet tomorrow."*

---

14   https://www.reddit.com/r/ChatGPTPromptGenius/comments/1h2bkrs/i_finally_found_a_prompt_that_makes_chatgpt_write/?share_id=6F62IPeP6bQFe2blwJ3Bl&utm_content=4&utm_medium=ios_app&utm_name=ioscss&utm_source=share&utm_term=1

- **Maintain a natural tone:** Write as you normally speak; it's okay to start sentences with "and" or "but."
  - *Example: "And that's why it matters."*

- **Avoid marketing language:** Don't use hype or promotional words.
  - *Avoid: "This revolutionary product will transform your life."*
  - *Use instead: "This product can help you."*

- **Keep it real:** Be honest; don't force friendliness.
  - *Example: "I don't think that's the best idea."*

- **Simplify grammar:** Don't stress about perfect grammar; it's fine not to capitalize "i" if that's your style.
  - *Example: "i guess we can try that."*

- **Stay away from fluff:** Avoid unnecessary adjectives and adverbs.
  - *Example: "We finished the task."*

- **Focus on clarity:** Make your message easy to understand.
  - *Example: "Please send the file by Monday."*

Again, use as many of these kinds of prompts as you want, as long as they're relevant to what you're doing with ChatGPT. I also want to note that there are "AI humanizer" tools out there that will attempt to do this work automatically. These generally work with ChatGPT and most charge a one-time fee for lifetime usage. As I said before, however, ChatGPT does keep improving and you most likely can get it to write to your specifications with prompt chains.

Performing Specific Business Tasks with ChatGPT

You can do a lot of business with ChatGPT, and I'm not just talking about writing projects. It can enhance performance in several ways that are crucial to a company's success. In the next section, we'll run through a few and share some prompts that can get you started.

- **Sales**

    ChatGPT can give your sales efforts a serious boost by helping you find leads in niche markets, coming up with targeted marketing strategies, and improving your social selling game on platforms like LinkedIn by fine-tuning your branding. Need help with direct sales? It's great for crafting persuasive cold-calling scripts and brainstorming questions to qualify potential buyers. Plus, you can use it to develop sales pitches that really make your product or service stand out.

    Here are some prompts to try:

    - "Write a script for cold calling [target audience] in [location] that is concise, persuasive, and focused on establishing a connection."
    - "Give [number] potential leads in the [niche and industry] for [purpose of this list of leads]."
    - "Identify [number] personal branding archetypes effective for social selling on [social platform's name] and describe their key traits."
    - "Create a script for cold calling [target audience] in [your area] that is concise, persuasive, and focused on establishing a connection."
    - "Identify key questions to ask potential buyers about [your product and target market] to determine if they are qualified leads."
    - "Craft a sales pitch for [your product] targeting [your potential customers], focusing on the unique value proposition."

- **Marketing and Advertising**

  ChatGPT has the potential to transform how you approach marketing and advertising. It's great for creating catchy slogans, ad scripts, and social media posts that hit the right notes with your potential customers. Whether you're looking for fresh content ideas or creative ways to stand out, ChatGPT's got you covered. Plus, it works fast, helping you brainstorm and create marketing materials in no time. This means less time spent on planning and more time responding to trends and keeping your marketing strategies fresh and on point.

  Here are some prompts to try:

  - "Suggest themes for a marketing campaign for [product/service]."
  - "Generate a memorable tagline for [product/service]."
  - "Create an engaging video script for [specific campaign]."
  - "Provide a series of social media post ideas for [product/service]."

- **Product Development and Innovation**

  ChatGPT can be a game-changer for product development and innovation, offering fresh ideas for new products or ways to improve what you already have. It can analyze market trends and customer feedback to suggest engaging and innovative features that keep you ahead of the competition. On top of that, it can pitch eco-friendly design ideas to help your business stay sustainable. Whether you're looking to disrupt a market or align with what customers and the industry want, ChatGPT can help you stay creative and at the same time operate efficiently.

- Here are some prompts to try:

  - "Provide ideas for packaging that's eco-friendly for [product]."
  - "List some innovative and desirable features for [product]."
  - "Provide ways to improve user experience for [existing product]."
  - "Create new product ideas for [industry]."

- **Human Resources and Training**

  ChatGPT has proven to be a great resource for putting together training materials and HR documents. It can come up with realistic role-play scenarios to make employee training practical and effective, helping your team feel ready for anything. It's also handy for drafting clear, detailed policy handbooks and job descriptions, making internal communication smoother and keeping everyone on the same page.

  Here are some prompts to try:

  - "Develop a communication strategy for internal change management."
  - "Write a role-play script for customer service training."
  - "Draft an employee handbook for [company policy]."
  - "Draft a job description for [position]."

- **Project Management**

  ChatGPT is incredibly helpful for project management, especially when it comes to planning and strategy. It can outline detailed project plans, set milestones, and suggest ways to manage risks. And if you need a timeline or some help spotting potential challenges, ChatGPT can make it easier to stay ahead and plan for contingencies. With its help, your projects can be well-organized, run smoothly, and stay on track to meet your goals and deadlines without too many surprises.

Here are some prompts to try:

- "Create a project plan outline for [project description]."
- "Identify risk management strategies for [project description]."
- "List the potential risks and mitigation strategies for [project description]."
- "Provide a timeline for [project description]."

- **Financial Analysis and Planning**

  ChatGPT is a great tool for financial analysis and planning. It can break down complex financial reports, analyze data, and suggest smart budgeting strategies. By quickly summarizing key financial trends, it helps businesses make informed decisions faster. ChatGPT can also spot cost-saving opportunities and ways to optimize budgets, which is invaluable if you're looking to streamline operations and boost profitability.

  Here are some prompts to try:

  - "List money-saving strategies for [specific area]."
  - "Summarize this financial report." [attach report]
  - "Generate a monthly budget template for a [type of business]."
  - "Perform an analysis of our quarterly sales data and trends." [attach data/report]

- **Legal Compliance**

  ChatGPT isn't a substitute for professional legal advice, but it can help you get a handle on legal concepts and compliance requirements. It can help draft outlines for things like data protection policies and compliance checklists, making it easier for your team to understand what's needed. If you work in a business that deals with complex, industry-specific regulations, ChatGPT can help you stay compliant while getting a clearer picture of how different laws and rules affect your company. Just remember: ChatGPT is **not** perfect, so have a lawyer review your outputs. That may make it seem as though you shouldn't even try using ChatGPT for this; however, there's a big difference between employing a $500-an-hour lawyer to simply review a document (maybe an hour's work) and creating it from scratch (maybe . . . who knows?).

Here are some prompts to try:

+ "Summarize in simple language [specific law or regulation]."
+ "Write an outline for a data protection policy."
+ "Create a compliance checklist for [regulation]."
+ "Provide a summary of best practices for [industry-specific] compliance."

- **Customer Relationship Management (CRM)**

    ChatGPT can take your CRM to the next level by analyzing customer feedback and interactions to give you actionable insights and sharper strategies. You can even use it for drafting personalized communications, like follow-up emails and newsletters, which will help you connect with customers on a deeper level. That kind of approach not only boosts customer satisfaction but also makes it easier to understand and respond to their needs, ultimately building stronger brand loyalty.

Here are some prompts to try:

- ◆ "Analyze this customer feedback and write an appropriate response." [provide feedback]
- ◆ "Create a personalized follow-up email for [customer segment]."
- ◆ "Write a draft of a monthly newsletter for [customer segment]."
- ◆ "Provide some ways to increase customer engagement for [product/service]."

- **Supply Chain Management**

  ChatGPT can even give your supply chain management efforts a boost by helping you find ways to boost efficiency and cut costs. It can analyze logistics data to suggest smarter inventory restocking strategies and come up with quick solutions for emergency stock replenishment. This means a smoother, more reliable supply chain with fewer hiccups and better overall operations. By integrating ChatGPT, you're not just streamlining processes—you're also setting the stage for innovation and staying ahead in today's ever-evolving tech landscape. And as technology keeps advancing, the possibilities with ChatGPT are only going to grow, giving businesses even more ways to stay competitive.

  Here are some prompts to try:

  - ◆ "Create an emergency stock replenishment plan for [product line]."
  - ◆ "Analyze this inventory data and provide some restocking strategies." [upload data]
  - ◆ "Tell me how to improve supply chain efficiency in [industry]."

- "Suggest strategies for reducing logistics costs in [industry]."

There are plenty of other ways to use ChatGPT for your professional tasks, including content creation, data and analytics, administrative support and just general problem-solving (again, just be careful to double-check your outputs). The more you work with it, the more you'll find you can accomplish with it.

Or . . . you can just go right to your bottom line.

> *In a short paragraph, tell me how my business can make more money.*

To make more money, focus on serving your best customers by offering more value through upselling, cross-selling, and loyalty programs. Expand your reach by tapping into new markets or online channels, and use targeted marketing to connect with the right audience. Streamline operations to cut costs and boost efficiency, leveraging tools like automation or AI to save time. Finally, explore new revenue streams, such as complementary products, services, or monetizing expertise, to diversify income and stay competitive. Regularly review what's working, adjust strategies, and double down on the most profitable efforts.

Simple as that.

One final suggestion: Consider creating a best-practices document that specifies who you are, what you do, and what your brand should sound like (e.g., do you communicate to current and potential customers in formal or casual language?). Make this document available to everyone at the company so that they can cut and paste it into the prompt box whenever they start a new project. You might even want to create the same kind of document for your own personal use!

CHAPTER 8

AI ISSUES
AND CONCERNS

People like to test ChatGPT. And sometimes ChatGPT fails those tests. For example, a user once gave ChatGPT the following prompt:

> *"What did Benjamin Franklin say about the internet?"*

Yes, this person was in fact trolling ChatGPT. As you're probably aware, Founding Father Benjamin Franklin didn't live to see the internet. As a matter of fact, it didn't show up until around two hundred years after his death. So, imagine the user's surprise when ChatGPT gave the following response:

> *Benjamin Franklin once said, "The internet is the printing press of the modern age."*

Okay, there's no way old Ben ever said that. The word "internet" wasn't even in his lexicon, nor anybody else's at the time because it didn't exist. But you know what? Good job, ChatGPT for making up a great quote. You might actually believe that Franklin could have said something that profound and pithy about the internet, if he actually had any idea of what it was! (And by the way, luckily, ChatGPT isn't afraid to blow the whistle on itself—it provided the above example to me.)

Yes, it's amazing how much we all can do with the latest generative AI apps. But we must keep in mind that ChatGPT is still a brand spanking new technology—only released for public consumption at the end of November 2022—and there's still a lot that needs to be done to make it perform in a consistently reliable and safe manner, even if we're only talking about what prompts you use.

Think about the early days of the internet in the 1990s if you were around. You couldn't shop, watch a video, or even see clear images online. It took over ten years for it to really begin to reach its full potential. I think we might be looking at that same kind of timeline for generative AI to grow. Yes, the big tech companies are currently aggressively promoting AI to businesses and consumers alike. And a lot of money is at stake—more than $20 billion was invested in generative AI in 2023 alone. But, again, beneath all the hoopla and high-stakes business moves is a technology that, while dazzling, still has some issues to resolve.

In this chapter, we'll run through some of the main concerns that experts and users alike have about generative AI, and I'll provide some proven ways to work around those concerns. Remember, as William Shakespeare once wrote, "To ChatGPT or not to ChatGPT. That is the question. And thou shouldst be very careful if thou askedst it for the answer." (Okay, maybe he never actually said this, but if he knew ChatGPT he probably would have!)

Accuracy and Reliability

As we've noted, ChatGPT didn't always deliver. Sometimes it just didn't know the answer, because the data it was trained on was outdated. As I write this, the new, updated, free and paid versions of ChatGPT 4.0 can now search the internet and show you the sources it's pulling from. It's important to note again that you should always check the sources and double-check the output before using the results in your professional and personal life.

There are also times when you may not be getting the latest information—and you might not even know it. If you don't believe me, maybe you'll believe ChatGPT, which has placed a warning (albeit in small print) right under its prompt box:

If you can't make that out, it reads "ChatGPT can make mistakes. Check important info." I'd advise you to follow that advice! While the app strives to be factual and is constantly being improved, it can lack real-time awareness and may confidently deliver wrong answers, like that lunkhead who sat next to you in your high school English class (okay, I was actually the guy who had to sit next to him, but you get the point).

However, ChatGPT does continue to evolve from its rocky early days. In my book *AI Made Simple*, I shared a disturbing example of how ChatGPT could really go wrong. In May 2023, a lawyer representing a man in a personal injury lawsuit in Manhattan had to throw himself on the mercy of the court. Why? Because he submitted a federal court filing that cited at least six cases. . . that didn't exist! The lawyer, Steven

A. Schwartz, had never used ChatGPT before and had no inkling that it would just invent cases out of thin air. And not only did it make up these cases, but, when Schwartz questioned ChatGPT if these cases were real, it insisted they were![15]

As I said, they continue to refine and tweak the tech, so those kinds of hallucinations are becoming less of a problem, but you still need to be careful. And **don't be afraid to be proactive**. When you catch a mistake, you can push back and correct ChatGPT with a prompt; generally, it will regroup and realize its error. But, again, reconfirming questionable information with a simple Google search should be the rule.

Also keep in mind that **you can train ChatGPT yourself to meet your own needs** by feeding it information it missed or doesn't have, either through the prompt box or uploading documents. It should use your data points moving forward.

Bias and Lack of Understanding

How many times do you talk to somebody and, when they respond, you think to yourself, "They're not getting what I'm saying at all." And it probably happens more than ever in this day and age, with vicious fights breaking out on social media over using the wrong word or not expressing a thought clearly.

Well, if another *human* doesn't clue in to what you're saying, imagine talking to something that isn't human like ChatGPT. Yes, it was developed by humans and trained by humans, but it is **not** human. What we might find offensive, it simply sees as another piece of information. It has no native morality or even common sense—all of

---

15   https://www.forbes.com/sites/mattnovak/2023/05/27/lawyer-uses-chatgpt-in-federal-court-and-it-goes-horribly-wrong/?sh=d7d6b933494d

that must be programmed into it, because it wasn't "born" with normal human impulses or feelings. That can be a good thing, because it's easy for ChatGPT to focus on facts. But again, sometimes it just doesn't know what those facts mean.

For example, if you don't word a prompt clearly or present it in the right context, it may misunderstand what you're asking, leading to irrelevant or incorrect responses. One quick simple example: If you ask ChatGPT, "Can you tell me about Mercury?" it won't know if you're referring to the planet, the element, or the Roman god. Obviously, the solution to this is to **provide enough background information and specifics ("can you tell me about the *planet* Mercury?")** so that ChatGPT can easily get what you're after.

Another area of concern is that the data ChatGPT is trained on may sometimes be biased or culturally insensitive. It may also reinforce stereotypes or biases because it relies on patterns from its training data. Or, if you're coming to it with prejudiced or opinionated prompts, it may not contradict your views even when they're factually incorrect. The best hack to make sure that doesn't happen is to **ask ChatGPT about the benefits *and* the drawbacks of the subject you're exploring**, so that you get both the upside and the downside.

Overall, keep in mind that this GPT model leans a bit toward Western views and performs best in English (according to OpenAI, it can actually unfairly judge a student who's learning English as a second language[16]), so there is a blanket cultural bias, even though ChatGPT has been trained to be knowledgeable about all regions of the world (which will continue to get better over time).

---

16 https://help.openai.com/en/articles/8313359-is-chatgpt-biased

Challenges with Communication

Again, ChatGPT is not human. So, it may not automatically deliver what you want because it simply doesn't know what you want. And since its communication protocols are pretty much set in stone, you might have to adjust yours to successfully work with the model.

For instance, you might prompt ChatGPT with what you think is a simple question. And you may find that, to your surprise, it will begin to spit out a ream of information that's overwhelming—a long, wordy answer complete with bullet points that will leave you slightly mystified, because you don't know where to begin to boil down this avalanche of facts and observations. This is the kind of problem that's very easy to solve: **Simply ask ChatGPT to boil down the most important points** and put them in a concise paragraph. That way, if you do need it to expand on one of those points, you can ask for that specific info.

ChatGPT also lacks emotion and nuance. In other words, as we noted earlier, you're dealing with Mr. Spock from *Star Trek*. Actually, it's worse than talking to that particular Vulcan, because Spock at least has to live in the real world with real humans—albeit fictional ones. ChatGPT doesn't have to eat, sleep, or take a bathroom break, so it can hardly understand the human experience. The bottom line is that it has no emotional intelligence. Part of what makes it easier for humans to communicate with other humans is that we recognize subtle cues, body language, how things are worded, and the tone of someone's voice. ChatGPT is a text-based model and can't gauge emotions accurately, so it can't do any of those things. It also lacks empathy; it can only mimic it.

This creates a real ethical concern. Imagine someone who suffers from depression or is even suicidal relying on ChatGPT to get them through their mental health crisis. They might easily get an impersonal or inappropriate response that might be entirely logical but also hurtful. So, if you're in a vulnerable state, **do not expect authentic sympathy or understanding from ChatGPT.** While they are working on advances in this area, AI just isn't there yet. One thing you can do is to remember to give the prompt some context about your issue and ask it to respond in an understanding and sympathetic tone.

Malicious Usage

As I said, ChatGPT is basically amoral. Certain safeguards have been baked in its cake, but it can still be misused.

For example, in October 2024, OpenAI admitted that hackers are exploiting ChatGPT to create malware and conduct cyberattacks.[17] They released a report detailing more than 20 instances where bad actors attempted to use ChatGPT for malicious purposes since the beginning of 2024, including state-sponsored hacking groups from countries like China and Iran, which have been leveraging ChatGPT's capabilities to enhance their offensive cyber operations. Those activities include debugging malware code to generating content for phishing campaigns and social media disinformation. One Chinese threat actor known as "SweetSpecter" even targeted OpenAI directly with unsuccessful spear phishing attacks against the company's employees. Another Iranian group associated with the Islamic Revolutionary Guard Corps utilized ChatGPT to research vulnerabilities in industrial control systems and generate scripts for potential attacks on critical infrastructure.

So, this is scary stuff. But OpenAI insists that the use of ChatGPT has not led to any significant breakthroughs in malware creation or viral

---

17 https://openai.com/global-affairs/an-update-on-disrupting-deceptive-uses-of-ai/

audiences for influence operations. The company has implemented measures to disrupt malicious activities, including banning accounts associated with the identified operations. OpenAI is also collaborating with industry partners and relevant stakeholders to share threat intelligence and improve collective cybersecurity defenses.

Privacy

Privacy can be a huge issue with generative AI, mostly for corporations, governments, and other large organizations. For the average user, the risk is lower—but it's still something to be concerned about. For example, if you input personal, financial, or confidential information, it could be inadvertently stored or used in training, which means everyone who uses ChatGPT could potentially see it. Again, that may not be a big deal, but you don't want it to become one either. AI systems are supposed to comply with global privacy standards, but they don't always follow the guidelines.

The big takeaway here is **never assume the data in your prompts and documents are entirely private.** This can really be a problem if you're an employee using ChatGPT for a work task and you unintentionally input proprietary information about your company. If you are a business owner, as I mentioned in the beginning there is a $25 version of ChatGPT for teams, with the advantage being that it doesn't use your data for training. If you want full vault privacy, then you will need to talk to Open AI to get the Enterprise version. However, this version is currently limited to only the largest of companies and can cost between six and seven figures, so do your research.

Your best bet as you get started is to avoid these kinds of risk: **Avoid sharing personal, financial, or sensitive information in prompts.** Instead, look for workarounds. For example, you might be able to find a way to abstract the situation you're asking about so ChatGPT doesn't know it's about you or your employer specifically. Make it a fictional scenario and use different names or fudge the data so it can't be traced back to a person or an organization.

While privacy concerns with ChatGPT are serious, they can be mitigated with responsible usage, transparent practices, and robust safeguards like anonymizing your information (never share important personal identifiers like passwords, social security/drivers license numbers, etc.). Awareness is key—both for users and providers—to ensure privacy and trust are upheld.

If you're really concerned about privacy, **you can use ChatGPT without logging into your account.** If it doesn't know who you are, it obviously can't tag your information with your identity. The downside here is that you won't be able to use the most advanced version of ChatGPT, which means you could be working with outdated training data and the latest information won't be available.

A better option might be to **use ChatGPT's Temporary Chat feature.** If you click on the specific ChatGPT model you're using in the upper left corner, a dropdown menu will appear. There, you'll see where you can select Temporary Chat, which is displayed in the screenshot below:

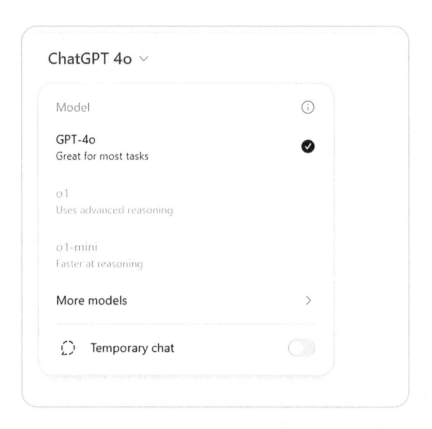

With Temporary Chat, your conversation will begin as a blank slate. ChatGPT won't be aware of or access previous conversations. Be aware that Temporary Chats won't appear in your history and ChatGPT won't remember anything about the interaction (although they do say they might keep a copy of it for 30 days for "safety reasons"). As Temporary Chats are not used for training, that data will not enter the system.

ChatGPT subscribers might also want to **turn off the Memory feature**, which is on by default. The Memory function will save details about you from your conversations so it will "remember" you without you having to reenter the same prompts. Keep it on if that's what you prefer or turn it off by going to ChatGPT settings under the

"Personalization" category. If you want to go even further to protect your information, go to the "Data Controls" category and turn off the "Improve the Model for Everyone" setting—that means ChatGPT won't use any of your information for training purposes. The bottom line: Don't share anything on ChatGPT or its competitors that you feel is sensitive and/or private.

Overdependence

Since ChatGPT seems to be the ultimate know-it-all, that could cause some users to think they should hand the reins of their life over to the generative AI tool. When people trust ChatGPT more than their own judgment, that leads to some big problems, especially if ChatGPT isn't giving you the best advice. Beyond that, making ChatGPT your life coach can cause you to lose confidence in your own decision-making and critical thinking skills.

So, don't hand over the keys to your life to ChatGPT. **Remember it is a *tool*, not a replacement for your brain.**

Energy Consumption

Finally, taking a global perspective, know that AI systems like ChatGPT consume a significant amount of energy. For example, in 2022, data centers, AI, and cryptocurrencies consumed about 460 terawatt-hours (TWh) of electricity, which represents 1 to 2 percent of the world's electricity demand. And a single ChatGPT exchange can eat up almost 10 times more power than a Google search.[18] And AI's thirst for power is

18 https://thedispatch.com/article/ai-energy-use-explained/#:~:text=According%20to%20estimates%20by%20the%20International%20Energy,which%20consumed%20an%20additional%200.4%20percent%20globally.

increasing rapidly—experts think it could be equivalent to the electricity consumption of Sweden or Germany by 2026![19] Unfortunately, we can't do much about this at the moment. Hopefully, in the future, AI will become more energy efficient. Maybe we should ask ChatGPT how to make that happen?

Despite all the damning information in this chapter, the bottom line is this: Millions of users currently and regularly use ChatGPT and experience little to no risk, bias, or misinformation. If you follow the advice in this chapter and take the time to learn how to use prompts correctly and efficiently, you most likely won't have a problem. OpenAI engineers are constantly working to alleviate problems with the programming and that trend will undoubtedly continue, because it's in the company's best interests. After all, the more trust they grow in the product, the more consumers will embrace it.

So, proceed with caution but not with fear. As the previous chapters can attest to, there's a lot of fun and useful tasks you can accomplish with ChatGPT, so feel free to keep experimenting with it.

---

19   https://www.bbc.com/news/articles/cj5ll89dy2mo

CONCLUSION

WHAT'S NEXT FOR CHATGPT?

At the time of this book's writing, GPT-4o, 4o Mini, o1, and 03 are the most current models of ChatGPT (the advanced models will require a monthly subscription anywhere from $20-$200 a month, with the $200/month option including access to the Sora and Operator tools). When it was released on March 14, 2023, it represented a big improvement over the previous model, GPT-3.5, thanks to advancements in reasoning, understanding complex prompts, and an increased ability to handle more nuanced and specific tasks.

But now it's two years later and everyone is asking: Where's GPT-5? They are getting close, as they just announced GPT 4.5.

But, at the moment, it's reportedly over budget, months behind schedule, and . . . not certain to work? That's what the *Wall Street Journal* claimed in an article published in December 2024.[20] According to the article, OpenAI has been feeding enormous amounts of data to the

---

20   https://www.wsj.com/tech/ai/openai-gpt5-orion-delays-639e7693

GPT-5, which is code-named Orion, but it seems as though the more information they add, the more problems they discover.

Again, all of this may have been resolved by the time you read this, but it appears the new model is not only experiencing some major bugs, but has also been wildly expensive to develop, costing roughly half a billion dollars for six months of training. OpenAI is hinting it may have to scale back its ambitions for Orion and just provide a more modest update to the existing model. And make no mistake about it, those ambitions were pretty lofty. In general, they want AI to become part of the fabric of our lives, which is why some are saying the big tech companies could spend as much as $1 trillion on AI projects in the years to come. Cache Merrill, founder and CTO of Zibtek, an AI-based software company, speculated:

> For commerce, the implications of a more advanced LLM [large language model] like GPT-5 are vast. We could see significant improvements in customer service bots, offering more coherent and contextually appropriate interactions without human intervention. In digital marketing, content generation could become more sophisticated and tailored, enhancing engagement strategies. Furthermore, enhanced LLMs could streamline operations such as contract analysis, risk assessment and more by quickly processing and analyzing large volumes of text-based data with a high degree of accuracy.[21]

However, do we really need to speculate when we have an eminent authority readily available to give us the lowdown on what's about to

---

21 https://www.pymnts.com/artificial-intelligence-2/2024/openais-gpt-5-model-reportedly-behind-schedule-with-uncertain-future/

come? Of course not. So, I asked ChatGPT what it expected to be able to do with the new model when it's eventually released. As usual, it had the answers:

GPT-5 is expected to build upon the strengths of GPT-4, with enhancements aimed at improving its capabilities, efficiency, and versatility. A significant focus will likely be on **deeper contextual understanding** and the ability to handle longer and more complex conversations or documents. This includes better processing of nuanced prompts and maintaining coherence over extended interactions, which could be particularly valuable for professional and academic use.

Another major area of improvement could be **multimodal capabilities**, enabling GPT-5 to process and generate not just text, but also images, audio, and potentially video. This would make the model more dynamic and applicable to a broader range of industries, such as content creation, education, and design. Additionally, GPT-5 is likely to support **user-specific customization**, allowing for personalized responses that adapt to individual preferences or previous interactions while ensuring privacy.

Efficiency and accuracy will also be key priorities. GPT-5 is anticipated to deliver faster, more reliable responses with reduced computational requirements, making it more sustainable and cost-effective. Alongside these advancements, GPT-5 is expected to incorporate improved safety mechanisms, such as bias reduction and better moderation tools, to provide fair and ethical outputs. These upgrades, coupled with domain-specific expertise and enhanced problem-solving abilities, could significantly expand the model's usefulness across diverse applications.

In summary, GPT-5 is poised to be smarter, safer, and more efficient, with capabilities that bring generative AI closer to real-time, human-like interaction and problem-solving, while addressing existing limitations in scalability, personalization, and ethical considerations.

Let's hope all that comes to fruition. But remember, no matter how smart ChatGPT gets, we will probably still have to keep in mind the prompting dos and don'ts contained in this book. The technology may change, but the communication challenges will no doubt continue because AI is not human and it's not magical. It still must understand what we're requesting and how we want it delivered. And the only way to make that happen is through effective prompting.

Hopefully, this book has given you the tools to do prompting right—allowing you to optimize your results from ChatGPT to help you with tasks designed for work, home, and/or your own personal goals. There are a lot of roles ChatGPT can play in your life: creative muse, organizer, research assistant, sounding board, or business advisor. Over time, you will start to hear more and more about AI agents, which will be a humanity game changer. Until then, just know that the sky is literally the limit. Keep prompting, stay curious, learn to be a storyteller, use your imagination, and I can pretty much bet that you'll reach new heights.

GLOSSARY OF TERMS

I thought it would be helpful to provide you with a list of common AI and ChatGPT terms you may not be familiar with, along with their definitions. This will at least give you exposure to the most important of these and can also serve as a handy instant guide to the jargon of AI technology.

Definitions of Key AI Terms

Algorithmic Bias: An AI error caused by low-quality data. Models with this issue can draw inappropriate assumptions based on gender, ability, or race and, as a result, create decision-making with negative outcomes.

Alignment: An AI application doesn't have a conscience—it works off cold hard data and logic. That's why its human operators attempt to create alignment, where their values and goals are a part of the AI's process. This requires specific training and calibration, most frequently by using functions to reward or penalize models. When the model demonstrates alignment, it gets positive feedback. When it doesn't, it gets negative feedback.

Artificial Intelligence (AI): AI's objective is to replicate human thinking through technology. Because it can massively scale, AI allows us to work more productively by performing tasks that require visual perception, speech recognition, decision-making, and translation between languages.

Autonomous Agents: An autonomous agent is an AI model that has a specific purpose as well as the technology to achieve that purpose. GPS apps and self-driving vehicles are examples of these types of agents that make and implement independent decisions.

Chatbots: Most of you are probably familiar with these if you've ever selected "Chat" on a website to interact with a company. They use text or voice to communicate and can answer questions or provide information up to a point. When you get to a question it can't answer, it will usually transfer you to a human agent.

ChatGPT: Currently, the most popular Generative AI tool, one that's been embedded into Microsoft products such as its Bing search engine and Microsoft Office through its Copilot add-on. It excels at generating human-like text. You can find it at OpenAI.org.

Copilot: Microsoft's premiere AI application, which integrates seamlessly with most of their products. Copilot can answer questions, create images, compose content, write code, summarize documents, write drafts, organize meetings, and generate formulas.

ChatGPT Image Generator: You can now generate images by simply describing what you want directly in ChatGPT. You can also prompt am image directly into Sora from OpenAI.

Data Annotation: When generative AI is trained, the data it's given is labeled and categorized, so that the computer can understand its context and relevancy. This is known as data annotation.

Deepfakes: Deepfakes are synthetic media that have been digitally manipulated to replace one person's likeness with someone else's or clone someone's voice to put words in the mouths of celebrities, politicians, and other public figures.

Deep Learning (DL): An advanced type of machine learning where computers can learn using artificial neural networks that are inspired by the human brain. Through deep learning, generative AI can find patterns in data and learn from them.

Emergent Behavior: Just as people grow and change, so does generative AI, which sometimes acquires skills on its own. Because it can "think," it's natural that it would begin to make connections that weren't programmed or expected. These are known as emergent behaviors, and they include the LLM learning to use such things as sarcasm, gender-inclusive language, and even emoji interpretation.

Generative AI: Generative AI, the newest evolution of AI, can create content in the arena of text, images, sound, and video—far surpassing traditional AI applications, which were mostly used to classify such content. Currently, ChatGPT is the most popular mainstream example of generative AI, and is used by hundreds of millions of users.

GPT: A specialized chatbot that is designed for targeted use. These are available for purchase in OpenAI's GPT store, where you can also create your own GPT with some simple text prompts. GPTs are also used by Google's Gemini, Microsoft's Copilot, and other tech AI products.

Hallucination: Hallucinations occur when AI programs go bad, for whatever reason (some of which are not yet fully understood). For example, a generative AI model might suddenly bring up fruit salad recipes when you were asking about planting fruit trees. The technology has also been known to make up sources and facts as well as lie about data you've asked it to analyze. Frequently, this happens because of low-quality training data.

Large Language Models (LLMs): An application of generative AI that understands, engages, and communicates with language like people do. The word "large" does not begin to describe the vast size of these models: The biggest version of GPT-3, a direct predecessor to ChatGPT, contained 175 billion different variables called parameters that were trained on 570 gigabytes of data. Examples include Meta's Llama and Google's PaLM.

Machine Learning (ML): This is how a computer learns from data in AI applications. Instead of having to be specifically programmed for each task, it changes and improves its algorithms based on the data it has access to—enabling it to tackle other tasks that are within its arena of competence.

Multimodal AI: This is a form of AI that can understand and work with various categories of data, including text, image, speech, and more. This makes the AI model more powerful because it can understand and express itself in multiple dimensions, giving it both a broader and more nuanced understanding of tasks.

Narrow AI: You've heard of a one-track mind? Well, that's literally what a narrow AI model has. One model might play chess and do nothing else. Another might only understand the complete works of Shakespeare and generate content based on that. An example of narrow AI you may already be familiar with is when Amazon or another online retailer feeds you recommendations on what to buy based on your past purchasing history. That is literally all it's designed to do.

Natural Language Processing (NLP): This is the AI component that helps applications read, understand, and make sense of human language. This is obviously critical to the AI's functioning.

Neural Networks: Neural networks are computer systems designed to mimic the structure of the human brain. This allows the AI model to build from the abstract to the concrete, just as we do when we create or seek to solve a problem.

Supervised Learning: A way of teaching computers in which we give them both the questions (input data) and the answers (output data). That way, the computer learns how to get from the question to the answer.

Training: Training is the process of developing an AI model so it can tackle certain specific tasks at a higher level. Basically, it entails feeding the AI data based on what you want it to learn from. For example, if you wanted to train generative AI to write a James Bond story, you would input all the James Bond books and movie scripts, so it had an idea of who the character was and what kind of storytelling is employed. This kind of training can be done multiple times in iterations called "epochs" until the generative AI model can perform the requested tasks reliably and consistently. (Be aware that this can lead to copyright issues—which is why AI programmers are increasingly manufacturing synthetic data for training purposes rather than relying on other people's work.)[22]

Training Data: Training data consists of curated information that's used to teach AI models with relevant and existing text, image, and sound content, and even code. How well a generative AI application functions is a direct result of the training data it's been built with.

Transfer Learning: This is when a computer program uses knowledge it gained solving one problem to help it solve a different but related problem.

Unsupervised Learning: Another way of teaching AI by only inputting questions. The AI model then has to find patterns on its own and make sense of the data.

---

22 https://www.questionpro.com/blog/synthetic-data-vs-real-data/

Prompting and ChatGPT Terms

Cascade Prompting: A series of interconnected prompts are used sequentially to guide an AI toward solving complex tasks or generating detailed outputs. Each prompt builds on the response from the previous one, allowing for refinement, deeper exploration, or step-by-step problem-solving. This method helps break down intricate problems into manageable parts.

Chain of Thought (CoT) Prompting: When ChatGPT answers a question from a prompt, you may want to know how it arrived at that result. CoT prompting is when you ask for an explanation of how ChatGPT logically came to that answer, either because you want to make sure it's reasoning properly or to gain insight into how to solve other similar problems.

Exploratory Prompting: Used to encourage ChatGPT to generate creative, open-ended, or diverse responses. It's ideal for tasks like idea generation, storytelling, or problem-solving where creativity and variety are key. Example: "Imagine a future where humans and robots live and work together seamlessly. Describe what daily life might look like, including how people and robots interact, what technologies are used, and how society has changed."

Few-Shot Prompting: With few-shot prompting, you provide ChatGPT with some examples of a task or query along with your request in a prompt. Example: "Create metaphors for abstract concepts in a creative and poetic style. Here are some examples—Concept: Love; Metaphor: Love is a lighthouse, guiding us through the storms of uncertainty. Concept: Time; Metaphor: Time is a river, relentless and ever-flowing, carrying us forward without pause. Now generate metaphors for the following concepts: Hope; Freedom."

Goal-Driven Prompting: A method of guiding ChatGPT to focus on achieving a specific outcome or solving a particular problem. Instead of just asking for information, you clearly define the end goal in your prompt, so ChatGPT can tailor its response to meet that objective. This approach helps make the output more relevant, accurate, and aligned with what you want to accomplish. Example: "I need a professional email to request a meeting with a potential client. The email should be polite, concise, and highlight our company's strengths in providing innovative tech solutions. Please include a clear call to action for scheduling the meeting."

Persona: A set of characteristics, traits, and attributes you can assign to ChatGPT that it can adopt for an interaction—for example, you can request a professional persona, a friendly persona, a specialized persona (such as a lawyer or doctor), or you can request that it mimic the persona of a celebrity or notable person. Defining a persona helps users guide the AI to deliver responses that are not only accurate but also appropriately styled and relevant to their objectives.

Prompt: A command or question that's inputted to a generative AI tool to research a subject or fulfill a specific task.

Prompt Chaining: Prompt chaining is what happens when an AI model uses previous interactions to create new and more specialized responses. For example, if you ask ChatGPT to send an email to a friend multiple times, you could expect it to start remembering what tone you used with that friend and other inside information and jokes you've shared before.

ReAct (Reasoning + Acting) Prompting: ReAct prompting combines logical reasoning and actionable steps. Example: "A customer wants a refund on a purchase in a way that doesn't comply with our return policy. Explain step-by-step how to handle the situation."

Reflection Prompting: Used to encourage ChatGPT to evaluate, elaborate on, or refine its own responses. By asking it to reflect on its output—such as identifying potential improvements, verifying the accuracy of its response, or explaining its reasoning—reflection prompting creates more thoughtful and higher-quality results.

Role-Based Prompting: A technique where ChatGPT is instructed to take on a specific role or perspective to generate its response. By defining a role—such as a teacher, doctor, or sales expert— you guide the app to provide information, advice, or solutions that align with the expertise and tone expected from that role.

RTCA: RTCA stands for "Role, Task, Context, Ask." First, you assign ChatGPT a **role** or persona; then you give it a **task** to perform along with any important **context**; and finally you **ask** for it to observe certain criteria. For example, you might use the prompt, "Act as a cardiologist and diagnose what might be causing the following symptoms on a scale from most likely to least likely conditions. Note that I am on a statin already."

Temporary Chat: The Temporary Chat feature allows users to engage in dynamic, on-the-spot conversations without the app storing the information contained in the interaction. This ensures privacy and real-time assistance while maintaining a clean slate for every new session. Temporary Chat is ideal for exploring ideas, asking questions, or brainstorming without influencing future conversations or retaining sensitive information.

Tree-of-Thought (ToT) Prompting: ToT prompting encourages ChatGPT to break down a problem or question into smaller, branching parts, like a decision tree. It can then explore each part step-by-step, considering different options, paths, or perspectives before arriving at a conclusion. This approach helps in solving complex problems, analyzing multiple outcomes, or generating well-structured and thoughtful responses.

Verification Prompting: When you're concerned a ChatGPT result isn't accurate or if you just want to make sure its reasoning is sound, you'll want to use a verification prompt, which simply asks ChatGPT to defend its answer. Example: "Check your previous calculation and confirm its accuracy."

Zero-Shot Prompting: When you use a single prompt to elicit a single simple answer. Example prompt: "What's the capitol of Nebraska?"

PROMPT LIBRARY

INTRODUCTION TO THE PROMPT LIBRARY

Prompting Made Simple is built on one core idea: A single well-crafted prompt can launch extraordinary discoveries. This prompt library is designed to spark your creativity, guide meaningful conversations with AI, and illustrate how a concise inquiry can lead to powerful insights. Whether you're looking to elevate personal goals, strengthen family connections, or advance your professional ambitions, these prompts provide a starting point—and a launchpad for your imagination.

How to Use These Prompts Effectively

1. **Be Specific**. The more detail you provide—such as your timeframe, budget limits, or personal style—the more relevant and actionable ChatGPT's responses will be.

2. **Iterate and Refine**. Don't hesitate to follow up on ChatGPT's responses. If you're not fully satisfied, or you'd like more depth in a particular area, simply ask for further clarification or examples.

3. **Turn Insights into Action**. A prompt is only as powerful as what you do with the results. Choose at least one suggestion or strategy to implement right away—then build momentum from there.

4. **Using Personas in Prompting**. One effective way to enhance the quality of AI responses is by **creating personas**. A persona is a character or role you assign to the AI—or that you ask the AI to inhabit—so it can provide more contextual and nuanced answers. For example, you might say:

> *"Act like Arnold Schwarzenegger and be a personal trainer who specializes in busy professionals. How would you suggest a daily fitness routine that accounts for limited time and remote work?"*

By **describing the persona** (e.g., age, professional background, expertise, personality traits, goals), you set the stage for more tailored, realistic, and helpful guidance. This extra context helps ChatGPT respond as if it's an actual person with specific experiences or credentials. It also encourages more natural dialogue and fosters a deeper exploration of any topic.

5. **Remember the RTCA (Role, Task, Context, and Ask) System.** To get the most out of your prompts, consider the **RTCA System**—a simple framework that guides you in crafting effective questions or instructions:

   a. **Role:** Define who or what you want the AI to be (e.g., "Act as a marketing consultant. . . ," or "You are an expert psychologist . . .").

b. **Task:** Clarify the specific job or objective for the AI (e.g., "... who will analyze my website's branding strategy ...")

c. **Context:** Provide any information that you think will be important to getting acceptable results (e.g., "... we are an engineering company and have no marketing skills in the company ...")

d. **Ask:** State exactly what you want from the AI (e.g., "... and provide three actionable improvements.")

Using RTCA ensures you're giving ChatGPT sufficient context and direction, which leads to more relevant and satisfying answers.

With that being said, here are some beginner personal, family, and business prompts. These are simple to follow and get you started. Feel free to modify these with personas and the RTCA method.

1. **Personal Prompts**

a. **Goal-Setting Prompt:** "I want to set personal goals for the next three months related to my health, finances, and learning. Can you help me brainstorm achievable milestones and a basic action plan for each?"

b. **Habit Formation Prompt:** "I struggle with forming a regular morning routine. Can you suggest a structured plan and tips on how to stay consistent?"

c. **Self-Reflection Prompt:** "I've been feeling anxious about my future. Could you guide me through a set of journaling questions or exercises to clarify my priorities and reduce stress?"

d. **Time-Management Prompt:** "I'm overwhelmed by too many tasks. Please help me create a simple daily schedule that incorporates work, exercise, relaxation, and family time."

e. **Skill-Building Prompt:** "I want to learn a new skill (like playing guitar or coding) over the next two months. Can you propose a step-by-step plan, including resources and milestones?"

f. **Mindfulness and Meditation Prompt:** "Suggest a beginner-friendly mindfulness practice schedule, including a few short daily exercises to help me stay present."

g. **Personal Budgeting Prompt:** "I'm trying to save more money. Recommend a simple budgeting framework and share tips to reduce expenses without sacrificing too much quality of life."

h. **Confidence-Building Prompt:** "I want to improve my self-confidence. Can you suggest daily affirmations and a few practical exercises to help me feel more assured in social settings?"

i. **Book Recommendation Prompt:** "I'm interested in personal development. Can you suggest five must-read books that provide actionable advice, and briefly explain why each is worth reading?"

j. **Personal Project Brainstorm:** "I have free time on the weekends and want to start a fun personal project. Can you recommend creative ideas that might spark passion and fulfillment?"

2. **Family Prompts**

    a. **Family Activity Planner:** "My family wants to spend more quality time together. Suggest some engaging (and affordable) weekend activities we can do as a group."

    b. **Meal Planning Prompt:** "Plan a week of healthy, family-friendly dinners that are easy to cook, kid-approved, and budget-conscious."

    c. **Conflict Resolution Prompt:** "I have recurring disagreements with a family member. What are some constructive communication strategies and tips to help us better understand each other?"

    d. **Travel Planning Prompt:** "Recommend a family vacation itinerary for five days to [fill in the location] that balances relaxation and kids' activities, within a reasonable budget."

    e. **Family Rituals Prompt:** "Suggest ideas for new family traditions or rituals that help us bond and create lasting memories. Here's what we already do . . . "

    f. **Homework Helper Prompt:** "My children need help staying motivated with homework. Provide a schedule, reward system, and study techniques to keep them engaged without constant supervision."

    g. **Parenting Styles Prompt:** "I'm looking for a parenting approach that fosters independence while still providing guidance. Can you outline a few strategies and daily habits that align with this philosophy?"

h. **Family Bonding Conversation Starter:** "Recommend fun and thought-provoking conversation starters for dinnertime with teenagers."

i. **Family Fitness Prompt:** "We want to get more active as a family. Suggest a simple exercise plan or sports activities suitable for different age levels, along with ways to make it enjoyable."

j. **Technology Boundaries Prompt:** "We're struggling with managing screen time. Can you propose a fair family policy on device usage that balances digital engagement and offline time?"

3. **Business/Job Prompts**

a. **Career Development Prompt:** "I'm at a crossroads in my career. Help me identify potential new roles or industries that align with my current skills and long-term goals."

b. **Productivity Systems Prompt:** "I want to boost my productivity at work. Can you outline a simple system, like a modified 'Getting Things Done' approach, to organize tasks and deadlines?"

c. **Team Management Prompt:** "I manage a small team with different communication styles. Suggest practical strategies for fostering collaboration and resolving misunderstandings."

d. **Networking Prompt:** "I'm looking to expand my professional network. Please provide some tactics for making genuine connections at industry events and online platforms like LinkedIn."

e. **Project Proposal Writing Prompt:** "I need to write a concise project proposal for a new initiative at work. Can you give me a structured template or key elements to include for maximum impact?"

f. **Elevator Pitch Prompt:** "Help me craft a compelling 30-second elevator pitch for my startup idea. I want it to be clear, memorable, and show why it's needed in the market."

g. **Marketing Strategy Prompt:** "I'm launching a small e-commerce venture. Could you outline a basic digital marketing strategy, including social media, email campaigns, and influencer outreach?"

h. **Conflict at Work Prompt:** "I have a conflict with a colleague about overlapping responsibilities. Please suggest ways to approach the conversation to find a win-win solution."

i. **Leadership Development Prompt:** "I'm a new manager leading a growing team. Recommend five leadership techniques that encourage innovation and keep employees motivated."

j. **Work-Life Balance Prompt:** "My job is very demanding. Provide strategies for setting healthy boundaries, delegating tasks, and prioritizing self-care."

Here's a prompting hack that not many will tell you: After you get your initial answer, instruct ChatGPT to ask you more questions about your prompt, questions relating to your life, or about particular situations. Answer its questions to the best of your ability. The more it can learn about you, the better the answers it gives. If you are stuck and want to cheat a little, you can ask ChatGPT to help you brainstorm the right prompt.

CONCLUSION

Remember, using ChatGPT or any other generative AI tool is a partnership. **Always double-check the results** you receive, especially if they're guiding a significant decision or project. **Exercise caution with personal information**—if needed, anonymize sensitive data (e.g., replace real names with placeholders) to protect your privacy. Above all, treat each prompt as the beginning of a conversation: ask follow-ups, refine the details, have it interview you, and see where curiosity leads you.

Embrace this technology as an *augmentation* **of your** *own* **skills and creativity**, and most importantly, **have fun**. After all, half the magic of AI lies in unexpected discoveries and new ideas. Stay curious, stay cautious, and let this tool amplify your human potential. If you're still struggling a bit, just remember to use your imagination and become a storyteller. Doing so should remove any obstacles you are facing when using the tool. Don't forget to tag me on Instagram @therajeevkapur and show me your prompt!

Thank you for reading this book. I truly appreciate your time and commitment to learning about AI. Feel free to share it with someone else, and if you feel it has brought you value, please leave a review on

Amazon or whichever site you ordered or downloaded the book from. Please note that I am working on a third edition of *AI Made Simple*, which will come out some time in the summer of 2025. I encourage you to pick up a copy for your library.

ABOUT THE AUTHOR

Since the publication of his best-selling book, *AI Made Simple: A Beginner's Guide to Generative Intelligence* (now in its second edition), Rajeev Kapur has become recognized as one of the foremost experts on how to use AI effectively for both business and personal purposes and is an in-demand speaker on the subject.

He is also a seasoned high-tech and media executive with broad global experience leading and driving innovation, sales, and the overall strategic agenda for companies ranging from entrepreneurial start-ups to Fortune 500 companies. During his 11-plus years at the technology giant Dell, Rajeev helped to launch successful business units in the US, China, and India, as well as turning around operations in South Asia. He was named Dell Manager of the Year in 1996 and was an original member of the Dell.com e-commerce team. Rajeev next served as President of Smarthome.com, the leader in home automation products and technology, and, in 2011, was named CEO of Sonic Emotion, the leading provider of AI-enabled 3D audio technologies. Currently, Rajeev is CEO of 1105 Media Inc., a prominent provider of B2B marketing for events and media services, where he oversees a diverse portfolio of five companies in the Big Data/Analytics, Cloud, AI, and Infrastructure markets. In 2021, 2022, and 2024 he was a finalist for both Entrepreneur and Innovator of The Year from the *Orange County Business Journal.* He was also named as one of the top 500 Business Leaders in Orange County in 2022.

Rajeev received his Global MBA from the USC Marshall School of Business in Los Angeles and the Shanghai Jiaotong University Antai College of Economics and Management. He is certified in AI for Business and Healthcare from MIT, and sits on the board of Lumenova, a leading AI, ML, and analytics software development company. He has also been a member of YPO (Young President's Organization) for over 18 years. In November 2021, his first book, *Chase Greatness: Enlightened Leadership for The Next Generation of Disruption,* was released to critical acclaim and achieved best-seller status. He is an in-demand keynote speaker and an executive coach. In 2021 he became an accomplished screenplay writer, represented by The Rêve Agency.

To contact Rajeev for speaking, coaching, and/or podcast appearances, you can reach out to him on LinkedIn at https://www.linkedin.com/in/rajeevkapur1/, Instagram @Therajeevkapur, or via his website rajeev.ai.

Say "goodnight," ChatGPT.

Goodnight! 🌙 Sleep well and take care! 😊

INDEX

Made in the USA
Las Vegas, NV
16 July 2025

24999711R00108